ENDORSEM

If there is one cry that reaches the heart of Abba, it is certainly the one that springs from the agony of a parent searching for their lost son or daughter. If there is one jubilation that rejoices the human heart and heavenly angels it is the turnaround and return of the one sought after. Jon and Jolene's Turnaround experience with their son is one of the greatest stories ever told. "Unto to us a child is born. Unto us a Son is given!" Sometimes God breaks into our world of pain and prayer in such extraordinary drama that we are awakened to the fact that it was sent and meant to become a God movement that touches the world. I'm convinced that Turnaround Tuesday is one of those prayer movements. Let faith explode in your heart as you read of the Christmas Day drama and the decrees that made a dream come true and could become the road of return to a million dreams come true.

Lou Engle
The Call, The Send
Lou Engle Ministries

When you read *Turnaround Decrees* by Jon and Jolene Hamill, faith begins to arise that anything going in the wrong direction can turn into God's destined path. The last time I was in Washington, DC, I gave a word about the need for turnaround. People hear the Word of God often, but Jon and Jolene hear the Word of God and then activate that Word into reality. *Turnaround Decrees* is an account of watching God turn around situations that are headed in the wrong direction and causing the best to manifest. Whatever situation you are in, this book will give you examples of how to decree the turnaround so your best is yet ahead.

Dr. Chuck D. Pierce
Glory of Zion International
Kingdom Harvest Alliance
Global Spheres Inc.

Voices that Can Be Heard! There comes a time when Authority is added to Revelation and it creates a "Voice that Can Be Heard"! It not only becomes a Voice that Can be Heard but it becomes a Voice that *must* be heard. That is exactly what has happened with the lives of the dynamic duo of Jon and Jolene Hamill. They are like a wrecking ball that tears down strongholds of the enemy and builds up a fortress of protection for Jesus Christ's sake. This is their greatest work in their finest hour.

James W. Goll
Founder, God Encounters Ministries and GOLL Ideation LLC
Franklin, Tennessee

This message is a "now word" spoken with clear prophetic insight and empowerment. It is a clarion call. While the destiny of nations, our nation, and the generations hang in the balance, now is the time for the warriors and the prophetic watchmen to arise. Many have felt themselves in a Jacob season of wrestling with the Lord— not wrestling from a place of struggle in our personal relationships with Him, but seeking His voice and direction on, How do we move forward? How do we pray? How do we engage in spiritual warfare and advance victorious in this season? How do we stand in the midst of government turmoil and shakings?

In this hour, the Lord is truly speaking Kingdom strategies of victory. That's what you will discover in this book. For all who are called to be an influencer in this Holy Spirit Era, this prophetic "now word" will give you the faith to resound with a "Yes, Lord! Here I am. I resolve to move forward to see the schemes of the enemy plundered and Your Kingdom awakening and harvest for both generations and nations manifest."

Rebecca Greenwood
Co-founder, Christian Harvest International
Strategic Prayer Apostolic Network

The hearts of the next generation need turning, and it's time for us all to turn back to the Lord in prayer and hotly pursue our loved ones. My dear friends of more than 20 years Jon and Jolene Hamill have written a prayer book that's a must-have for every family. Read this book and launch these prayers into action to set the captives free in your family, community, and nation. Those of you who contend for their loved ones to turn today can see them become burning lamps for the Lord forever.

Will Ford
www.818theSign.org
www.dreamstreamco.com
Author of *The Dream King: How The Dream of Martin Luther King Is Being Fulfilled To Heal Racism In America*

My friends Jon and Jolene Hamill have lived the forerunning message contained in their new book *Turnaround Decrees*. It is filled with firsthand accounts of how securing covenant becomes the foundation for seemingly impossible turnarounds. For those who long to see breakthrough secured for their families, cities, and nations, this book is both a roadmap and a training manual. You will discover the power of decrees sourced in covenant that bring about God's redemptive purpose and how to release them in your own life. May you be impacted as I was to see this Elijah mandate, turning the hearts of fathers back to their children, fully realized. It's turnaround time!

Chris Mitchell, Jr.
Founder, King's Gate International
Virginia Beach, Virginia

Many have wanted to change their past, wishing they could "right the wrongs" but hopelessly believing it wasn't possible. In *Turn-around Decrees,* you will find the hope to change the past and prepare for the future. We can be part of redeeming the timelines for our nation, our families, and our individual lives. This is a book of proven events that will give you tools to see the Kingdom of God and His covenant destiny come into place. Jon and Jolene's ability to communicate the events and provide a scriptural foundation is outstanding. They have been faithful carriers to redeem the time. This book, along with *Washington Watchmen*, are ones I highly recommend to advance your walk with God.

Dr. John M. Benefiel
Presiding Apostle, Heartland Apostolic Prayer Network
Presiding Apostle, Global Apostolic Prayer Network
Founder and Senior Pastor, Church on the Rock,
Oklahoma City, Oklahoma

Jon and Jolene have put in an encapsulated form a "Glory scroll" for us to swallow! Get this to the people! I am fired up to see these prophetic assignments and understanding come together.

True scribes of our day, Jon and Jolene have chronicled from a front-row seat the ebb and flow of the prophetic and prayer movements over these last 20 years. Now they are coming to define them. This book gives clarity and a solid direction for the 2022 campaign and beyond. It is a "Time Gate" script!

Candy Sunderland
Director, HAPN Alaska
Mountain Home Fellowship
Palmer, Alaska

Jon and Jolene share with the authority of authenticity in this timely, strategic book that is a gift to the global prayer movement as well as to those praying for America. We have walked together with Jon and Jolene for over 20 years, and prayed together to see some significant "turnaround" moments here in Israel. More than ever, we must not give in to the hopelessness that has been released against so many intercessors. This book will give you new hope, new courage, and new revelations to see mighty turnarounds in your family, city, and nation.

Rick & Patricia Ridings
Founder and Directors, Succat Hallel, Jerusalem, Israel

Similar to their previous books, in *Turnaround Decrees,* Jon and Jolene establish a concise, targeted revelation that empowers the entire Body of Christ. By masterfully knitting together our nation's inheritance, the word of the Lord, and the God-given dreams and visions, this step-by-step guide provides an equipping strategy and key markers to navigate the days, times, and seasons ahead. Through the decrees in this book you, too, will witness the Breaker breaking through and bringing transformation in your world.

Jamie & Redonnia Jackson
Founders and Senior Pastors, The Remnant Church,
Brunswick, GA

This whole book is a prophetic message that will change your life and give you keys for the turnaround for your family and life that you have been searching for.

Cindy Jacobs
Founder, Generals International
Presiding Apostle, Reformation Prayer Network,
Cedar Hill, Texas

Psalm 11:3 reminds us, *"If the foundations be destroyed, what shall the righteous do?"* This book, the latest masterpiece from Jon and Jolene Hamill, leads us to the answer.

Jon and Jolene Hamill's prophetic work has taken them from Washington, DC, to every state of our republic, as well as to Jerusalem. In their newest book, *Turnaround Decrees*, they cast a vision for a global movement to release God's turnarounds in the lives of individuals, nations, and families, turning the hearts of the fathers to the children and children to their fathers through "Turnaround Tuesday prayer." They lead us with mighty decrees and strategies from heaven's War Room. And they give many practical applications so you can gain consistent, proven results.

Jon and Jolene together have the pulse of the prophetic similar to the men of Issachar who "understood the times" (2 Chron. 12:32). They have stood on the wall and have been faithful to watch and warn—vigilant in their watching, and vigorous in their warnings.

I passionately appreciate Jon and Jolene's emphasis on the hidden power of covenant to unlock God's turnaround. As with Jon, my ancestor John Robinson was also among the Pilgrims whose legacy established America as a nation in covenant with God. Robinson was known as the pastor to the Pilgrims, mentoring them, sending them on their mission. Through the Return gatherings, government consultations, and other ministry work we are also intensively focused on keeping our treasured inheritance alive. It's the only way true freedom will remain. For this alone it is a must-read!

The heritage of Jon's DNA continues to flow from his distant relative Paul Revere as well, as a watchman for America's freedom. That said, an undelivered speech about freedom by John F. Kennedy seems hauntingly prophetic for our watch in history. On November 22, 1963, in Dallas, Texas, shots rang out as President Kennedy was assassinated. At 43 years of age, the youngest president ever elected also became the youngest president to die, after serving barely a thousand days. Kennedy was on his way to the Dallas Trade Mart to deliver a speech, in which he prepared to say:

"We in this country, in this generation, are—by destiny rather than choice—*the watchmen on the walls of world freedom*. We ask, therefore, that we may be worthy of our power and responsibility, that we may exercise our strength with wisdom and restraint, and that we may achieve in our time and for all time the ancient vision of peace on earth, goodwill toward men. ... That must always be our goal—and the righteousness of our cause must always underlie our strength. For as was written long ago, *Except the Lord keep the city, the watchman waketh but in vain*."

You and I are being called and equipped as watchmen on the walls of world freedom. Thank you, Jon and Jolene Hamill, for summoning us to arise.

Kevin Jessip
Co-Chair of The Return International
President of Global Strategic Alliance Ministries (GSA)
Sarasota, Florida

TURNAROUND
DECREES

DISRUPT THE ENEMY'S PLANS
& SHIFT YOUR CIRCUMSTANCE
INTO BREAKTHROUGH

TURNAROUND
DECREES

JON & JOLENE HAMILL

DESTINY IMAGE® PUBLISHERS, INC.

P.O. Box 310, Shippensburg, PA 17257-0310

"Promoting Inspired Lives."

This book and all other Destiny Image and Destiny Image Fiction books are available at Christian bookstores and distributors worldwide.

For more information on foreign distributors, call 717-532-3040.

Reach us on the Internet: www.destinyimage.com.

ISBN 13 TP: 978-0-7684-6217-3

ISBN 13 eBook: 978-0-7684-6218-0

ISBN 13 HC: 978-0-7684-6365-1

ISBN 13 LP: 978-0-7684-6219-7

For Worldwide Distribution, Printed in the U.S.A.

3 4 5 6 7 8 / 26 25 24 23 22

DEDICATION

THIS YEAR LAMPLIGHTER MINISTRIES celebrates 10 years of ministry to Washington, DC, and from Washington, DC, to the nation. The Lord is so faithful! What once seemed impossible has come to pass before our eyes. In the words of our forefathers, let the glorious Name of Yeshua have all the praise!

In Jesus, this book is dedicated to Bill and Marlene Brubaker, who served tirelessly as intercessors from Washington to Washington to Jerusalem, and as a mom and dad to the Lamplighter family.

Jolene and I also want to honor many other friends with similar passions, whose lives were also cut short in this season of challenge. Undoubtedly their work continues from the other side of the veil.

This book would not have been birthed without the visionary direction and friendship of Tina Pugh and Destiny Image; the vigilant intercession of Lori Perz and our amazing prayer team; and the capable oversight of Martin and Cindy Frankena, tasked with the impossible mission of keeping us on track. Special thanks to Mike and Cindy Jacobs and the ACPE, Jim and Becky Hennessey, and Lou Engle for launching with us this Turnaround Tuesday movement. Thank you, John Benefiel, Kevin Jessip, and Chuck Pierce, for providing key apostolic counsel. Thank you, Dutch and Ceci Sheets, for being there for us, for sharing dreams, and for writing the foreword.

Speaking of counsel, we'd also like to extend our profound gratitude to Russ and Julie Zylstra, as well as Tom and Lynnie Harlow, and our ever-capable home group, for your friendship, wisdom, revelation, and support.

We cannot fail to mention Chris Mitchell, Jr., Jamie and Redonnia Jackson, Shoshana (aka the "Isaiah 54 girl"), and many others whose efforts toward securing God's turnaround have made it into these pages. Thank you for your collaboration!

Finally, we want to honor all our friends and supporters across the nation, whose ceaseless vigil has helped keep our lamps burning to this day. No King but Jesus!

"It is for us the living, rather, to be dedicated here to the unfinished work which they who fought here have thus far so nobly advanced. It is rather for us to be here dedicated to the great task remaining before us—that from these honored dead we take increased devotion to that cause for which they gave the last full measure of devotion—that we here highly resolve that these dead shall not have died in vain—that this nation, under God, shall have a new birth of freedom—and that government of the people, by the people, for the people, shall not perish from the earth."

Abraham Lincoln,
The Gettysburg Address

CONTENTS

FOREWORD

MUCH HAS BEEN SAID OF LATE about the subject of "turn-arounds." Perhaps that's because we need them so desperately. Individuals, families, businesses, governments, churches, education systems—sadly, the list could go on and on—are all in desperate need of turnarounds. In America we kill babies, no longer know the difference between male and female, teach kindergartners that they can change their genders, elected a mentally declining president, distort and revise history, embrace socialism, spend trillions of dollars we don't have, keep strip clubs open while shutting down churches, censor truth while promoting lies, and other completely insane activities way too numerous to mention here. My purpose is not to shock you—I'm sure that, like me, you're way past that—but to state emphatically: WE NEED THIS BOOK!

The subject of spiritual "decrees" has also begun to increase in the Church, though not with the necessary level of understanding and participation. Holy Spirit has a plan to change this: The revelation meter is about to amp up. He is adding to our spiritual arsenal by bringing further insights regarding this important exercise. It's true that believers have long known the power of God's spoken words—they created the universe, after all. However, realizing the power of OUR words, when biblically based and inspired by Holy Spirit...well, that's been rarely understood.

This is about to change.

The prayer, prophetic, and apostolic movements of the last 40 years have caused a tremendous increase of revelation in the Church, and we are beginning to see the fruit of this. Seeds take time to grow, but Holy Spirit's seeds have now been planted. Their sprigs have broken through the soil, plants have formed, and fruit is maturing. The glad tidings of salvation announced at Christ's conception didn't materialize for 34 more years, and after much blood, sweat, and tears, I might add. So much for "instant gratification" turnaround. But as surely as the words of the Holy Spirit came to fruition then, they will today. It takes time for our Helper to restore truth and giftings to the Church. But you can rejoice in the fact that the fruit of what the Holy Spirit has been orchestrating over the last four decades is about to manifest. *Turnaround Decrees* will greatly aid this process.

There is a vast reservoir of untapped power in the womb of most believers, just waiting to be released. This "river of living water" (John 7:37-38) is filled with miracles, conversions, healings, deliverances, wealth, and numerous other descriptions of "abundant life" (John 10:10). And when its water merges with other wells and streams, the power multiplies into a nation-transforming dynamo. Make no mistake about it, the power to change the world resides in the womb of the Church, lying in wait for the spirit of revelation to awaken it.

And Heaven's alarm clock is about to sound.

This book, and I'm sure there will be many more released by Holy Spirit, is part of Heaven's reveille. The Captain of the Lord's Host has issued a command from Heaven, and Holy Spirit is releasing it on earth: "Wake up, Church! I need you to be who you are. You're My government on earth, My power agents, My ambassadors, My distributors."

Jon and Jolene Hamill have given us a brilliant, compelling, practical, and captivating tool. It will stir the pregnant waters of the strongest force on earth. The power in you will be unlocked as you read it, and you will see personal turnarounds. Just as importantly, Heaven's cause on earth will see turnarounds, as well. I guarantee it.

Dutch Sheets
February 6, 2022

A GODLY DEFIANCE

THIS IS A BOOK ON TURNAROUNDS—specifically how to partner with God to receive His turnaround, align with His turnaround, and decree His turnaround to impact your world. You probably would not be exploring these pages unless you were seeking a change in your trajectory from the Lord yourself!

Maybe you are seeking a turnaround for your loved ones, for your marriage, your health, your business, or for a deeper relationship with Jesus. The chapters ahead are packed with examples of dramatic, documented turnarounds manifested by His hand. Equally important, each chapter conveys proven biblical principles that will help you secure similar results.

Many of the strongest breakthroughs are intensely personal, and we share them with the goal of equipping you to overcome challenges in your own life and family. Turnaround time!

Above all, you will learn to make decrees from your position of kingship before God's throne, seated with Christ in heavenly places and ruling with Him to impact your world.

The nations will understand this clearly in the days ahead. You and I are now being granted a rare opportunity to both gain understanding and pioneer a new movement.

We are in an hour similar to the era of the American Revolution, except this time the authoritarian regime contending to steal our

freedom is actually embedded within our own government and culture. In this way, we have perhaps most closely resembled pre-World War II Nazi Germany.

Too extreme? Keep in mind Germany was a strong Christian nation, actually the birthplace of the Protestant Reformation, when it was taken over. Propaganda developed by the Nazis radically shifted their nation and culture away from their covenantal foundations, and toward dictatorship. More, the propaganda infused within many, youth especially, a welcoming of governance by dictatorship.

Keep this in mind: All totalitarian movements seek to indoctrinate coming generations. They target our children. This is happening here in America at a dramatically accelerated rate. And it puts in jeopardy those you love the most.

The good news is that the Lord is giving us a way not only to stem the tide but reverse it. It is against this backdrop that, in 2021, the Lord encountered me and again decreed a season of turnaround. As you will discover, this turnaround is on a personal level first, then to our nation and nations. We believe it will become the most comprehensive turnaround in modern history. For His glory! That is what this book is primarily about.

All this noted, our hour of history mandates godly defiance to forces seeking to define our future apart from God's desire. As Ben Franklin famously observed, "Rebellion to tyrants is obedience to God."

I am reminded of the courageous rabbi and his wife who lit a Hanukkah menorah in their window overlooking an oversized Nazi flag. Daniella Greenbaum wrote a powerful recounting for the New York Times. "In 1932, just before Hitler's rise to power, their menorah shone brightly for all their neighbors to see. Its light—and the meaning behind it—was made all the more incandescent given the symbol of Jew-hatred hanging from the building across the street."[1] According to the article, on the back of their Hanukkah a simple declaration was inscribed, borne of this act of godly defiance. Rachel Posner, the wife of renowned German rabbi Avika Posner wrote: "'Death to Judah' so the flag says. 'Judah will live forever,' so the light answers.'"

Friends, what is your own light speaking? As we embark on this journey through God's turnaround decrees, please know that your burning lamp is the ultimate decree. One small candle can still light a thousand. It overcomes all the encroaching darkness, if only you resolve to shine.

No King but Jesus!
Jon & Jolene Hamill
Washington, DC

PART 1

WHAT ARE
TURNAROUND
DECREES?

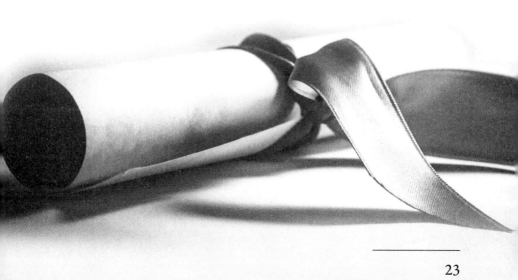

CHAPTER 1

TURNAROUND TUESDAY— A NEW MOVEMENT

"I kept watching, and that horn was waging war with the saints and prevailing against them, until the Ancient of Days came and judgment was passed in favor of the saints of the Highest One, and the time arrived when the saints took possession of the kingdom." (Daniel 7:21-22)

EARLY IN THE MORNING ON JULY 4, 2021 a scroll appeared before me (Jon) in a vision, hovering over our bed. It then unfurled. Similar to the Declaration of Independence and other historical parchments defining new eras for mankind, this scroll was golden brown and brighter in the middle than on the sides. It looked aged. But surprisingly it was completely blank.

During the vision of the unfurling scroll, I suddenly "knew" five things from the Lord:

Scrolls from Heaven are now being released with the potential to dramatically reshape our world. We have come to refer to these scrolls as "turnaround decrees." Tremendous authority is accompanying each turnaround decree to catalyze God's intended breakthroughs.

God's decrees frame the ages, the epochs, the eras. Just as "Let there be light" unleashed a new beginning for the world, so His decrees over your life can bring the light of dawn to your darkest hour, or your children's greatest challenge.

Which brings up the second point.

The blank scroll seen in the vision is being made available for each person who earnestly desires it. As with Queen Esther in her day, the Lord is inviting you to become an active participant in His rulership. This means that you and I have a vital role to play in securing these decrees, seeking Him for revelation, and then declaring words that change history.

> *"Now you write to the Jews as you see fit, in the king's name, and seal it with the king's signet ring; for a decree which is written in the name of the king and sealed with the king's signet ring may not be revoked"* (Esther 8:8).

The scroll appeared aged because the words which would soon fill it were not only going to impact the future, but the past. This third "knowing" imparted in the experience is fascinating. Through your efforts, the Lord's decree will become a bridge through which His healing connects with the past, the present, and the future all at once.

(Please note that you cannot escape your past. But you can actually repair it. In a *Back to the Future* way, you can repair your past to redeem your present—and restore His dream for your future. More on this soon.)

From this point on in the story of America, everything is new. That's another reason why the scroll is blank. It was as though the words of the Declaration of Independence, signed on July 4, 1776, were awaiting sequels that ensured the continuance of its legacy. Freedom has not changed. But the challenges we face to secure, protect, and defend our liberty have changed from the days of our nation's founders. Freedom decrees are now being issued to define the eras ahead.

But there was a warning attached to this knowing. I saw how malign forces seek to take advantage of this "time gate" for new beginnings to erase our independence, replacing it with a dominion of veiled totalitarianism disguised as "freedom," sourced in spiritual darkness. Literally a takeover. To accomplish their quest, these forces are first seeking to eradicate our covenantal legacy in God. The good news is that, at the very same time, Heaven's gates are open to help us realign covenantally with the decrees of our foundational liberties in a way that reconciles our past and empowers this precious gift for generations to come. Mark my words. Either we as a nation make this shift, or we will eventually yield to the enemy's intentions.

The anniversary of the signing of the Declaration of Independence, July 4, 2021, marked the date I was to begin writing *Turnaround Decrees*. The book began with this humble step of obedience.

I wonder if America's founders were at all intimidated by the specter of filling the empty space on the scroll we now know as the Declaration of Independence. History bears witness that they struggled, they argued, they prayed. Amazingly their sacred decree started a revolution and birthed a freedom nation, turning the known world order upside down. My prayer is that the unfurling of these scrolls today will grant you, and perhaps our nation, a similar window of opportunity.

Discovering the Power of God's Turnaround

Jolene and I have experienced miracles as we pursued God's turnarounds, at His direction. It all began in 2014 when we were directed by Holy Spirit to a passage of Scripture we have since come to call the "Turnaround Verdict." We gathered at Faneuil Hall in Boston on 7-22 to receive this Daniel 7:22 verdict. Historic Faneuil Hall is actually where many founders met to mobilize toward the American Revolution. And the gathering proved revolutionary for us. The trajectory for us personally, as well as for the nation, began to shift dramatically from that date forward. From Daniel 7: *"I kept watching, and that horn was waging war with the saints and prevailing against them until the Ancient of Days came and judgment was passed in favor of the saints of the Highest One, and the time arrived when the saints took possession of the kingdom"* (verses 21-22).

The "Turnaround Verdict" conveys a dramatic change of events. One moment the saints are being utterly defeated, while the next moment they are being released to possess the Kingdom. Wow, does that sound familiar to our world!

The process shown—approaching the Lord as the Ancient of Days, and securing His verdict in your favor—is central to unleashing the potential of Heaven's turnaround in your life and sphere.

So many miraculous interventions occurred immediately following the release of this verdict. Churches have come alive. Broken lives have been repaired. Physical healings have occurred. Lost people have discovered, or rediscovered, the power of their Redeemer. Longstanding promises seemingly stuck in a perpetual void have suddenly come to birth. The faithfulness of our God has become His real-time handiwork in everyday life, for all to see.

> The process shown—approaching the Lord as the Ancient of Days, and securing His verdict in your favor—is central to unleashing the potential of Heaven's turnaround in your life and sphere.

Not that all will celebrate. Some of God's greatest turnarounds, especially on a governmental level, have provoked unimaginable vitriol and resistance. Especially when their power base begins to shift. Yet still, the Kingdom has advanced.

It has been an incredible honor to experience so many of these turnarounds firsthand in Washington, DC, even at the White House, as we saw the

Lord move in response to relentless prayers. Many of our experiences are recorded in our previous book *White House Watchmen*. We saw the restraining of government-funded abortion, nationally and internationally. Economic resurgence has lifted all Americans to new levels of prosperity, especially women and minorities. Judges appointed to the Supreme Court and district courts have already begun to shift the judicial branch away from judicial activism and toward basic constitutional law. Collaboration with Israel replaced punitive measures against the Covenant Land. Even the US embassy was relocated to Jerusalem! And the Abraham Accords brought diplomatic breakthroughs once considered impossible. Freedom of religion was also significantly empowered, nationally and internationally. And so much more.

We cannot escape the fact that America suffered extraordinary collateral damage as well, due to challenges both within and without. Perhaps that's why consistent, strategic intercession was so sought after by many governmental officials. We'll explore all this more in the pages ahead.

But I will say unequivocally that many epoch-defining turnarounds came in concert with the Daniel 7:22 verdict for our land: judgment in favor of the saints, restraining the forces of darkness, and releasing the saints to possess the Kingdom. In short, turnaround!

Then suddenly it seemed as though the hand of God had lifted.

Our home is a watchman's perch that overlooks Washington, DC. From our condominium in Pentagon City, the White House, the Capitol, the Supreme Court, and the State Department are all in view. And we've been privileged to touch each of these spheres in a unique way. That said, in the first few months of 2020, from our vantage point it seemed like the grace to gain His turnarounds had stopped on a dime. Not that there weren't miracles or turnarounds anymore. But success was very tempered. Breakthroughs in governmental prayer that once seemed to come instantaneously became arduous and exhausting to attain.

Then came the onslaught of COVID-19. America masked up. The economy shook. Many of the Greatest Generation passed. The horrific death of George Floyd sparked protests nationwide as embedded racism became exposed. In major cities, movements to defund the police opened the gates wide for the largest crime wave in decades. Rioting and looting overtook our cities, even with entire blocks surrounding the White House succumbing to the scarring.

As COVID exploded, lawlessness exploded. The Trump administration fumbled. The Deep State gained. And our nation seemed to be thrust into an unstoppable downward spiral.

Then came the 2020 elections.

This brings up an important point. Though *Turnaround Decrees* stands completely on its own, it is written as a companion volume to our previous book *White House Watchmen*, published in the summer of 2020 by Destiny Image. A few challenges prophesied in *White House Watchmen* are now defining our world.

2017 Prophecy—Midnight Crises by 2020

In 2017 we prophesied that America was approaching a midnight hour and that by 2020 America would face a series of "midnight crises." A midnight hour for America. A midnight crisis. A midnight cry. A midnight turnaround. A midnight awakening. I also saw that how we confronted these crises and overcame them, would even become a roadmap for believers at the very end of days.

Of course, in 2017, we could not have imagined the onslaught of plagues, the unchecked rise of lawlessness, the influence of the deep state, and so much more. It's pretty clear that aspect of the word proved correct. Especially when you realize COVID-19 was first reported by China to the World Health Organization on December 31. By the year 2020, there will be a series of midnight crises...

For clarity's sake, we wrote our second book, *Midnight Cry*, around this "midnight crises" warning, and included it in *White House Watchmen* as well. *Turnaround Decrees* is the third book to highlight it. And I believe these together provide a sequential roadmap, equipping the Body of Christ to secure God's intended breakthroughs.

America is indeed in a midnight hour. The peril is real. Either we complete God's turnaround for our nation or intentional sabotage could soon become so comprehensive that it cannot be undone.

But here's some good news embedded in this very sobering warning we are now living out: The word of the Lord was clear that the opportunity remains open for you and me to not only confront the challenges but overcome them. And that's largely what *Turnaround Decrees* is about.

> America is indeed in a midnight hour. The peril is real. Either we complete God's turnaround for our nation or intentional sabotage could soon become so comprehensive that it cannot be undone.

Turnaround Movement Reset

In February 2021, a month after Joe Biden was inaugurated, the Lord initiated a series of 4 a.m. encounters where He showed me how His Daniel 7:22 turnaround movement is being released again from the throne. By revelation, I understood the turnaround movement would be initiated beginning Passover 2021 and grow through 2022 and beyond.

Given the circumstances, at first I simply could not grasp this. Nor could many of my friends. Many were honestly overwhelmed by circumstances which had seemingly defied our most persistent prayers. After giving our all, we were spent. Maybe you can identify!

But the clear revelation from the Lord continued. This fresh release of God's turnaround movement will be similar to the 2014 release, but even greater in scope in a way that will impact not only our nation's governance but the next generation in a defining way.

Amazingly we saw significant breakthroughs begin again from the moment we stepped out. We still have a long way to go. But already our world has changed!

The Hebrew prophet Zechariah was in a similar mindset when the Lord visited him over the restoration of a movement. In answer to the prayers of Daniel the prophet, a turnaround had been initiated by King Cyrus in a previous season. The Covenant People were granted passage back to Israel. Cyrus even decreed the rebuilding of Jerusalem, including the Temple and the city's walls. But this movement had been sabotaged literally by the "deep state" of their day, in open defiance of Cyrus' decree of restoration. Finally, the work had stopped altogether. For decades.

> *"And the angel of the Lord that was speaking with me returned and roused me as a man who is awakened from his sleep. And behold a lampstand"* (Zech. 4:1-2).

Biblically, the lampstand represents God's covenant and His covenantal presence. He saw the lamp being perpetually filled with fresh oil so it could continue burning. When the prophet asked about the meaning, the reply from Heaven was, *"Not by might nor by power, but by My Spirit, says the Lord of hosts."* (verse 6).

That's a word for us today!

Zechariah's awakening encounter became a sign of two things. First, a "time gate" was opening to finish the work that had been stopped. It was time to complete the turnaround!

Second, Heaven was pouring a perpetual stream of provision into the lampstand, more than enough oil for the menorah to burn continually. This symbolized the provision He was releasing to complete the Temple's rebuilding. Power to gain wealth to establish His covenant (see Deut. 8:18)!

Beginning Passover 2021, we began to prophesy the restoration of God's turnaround movement. It became time to complete the turnaround that He had initiated! And the word of the Lord began to manifest before our very eyes. The movement has only grown until this very day.

Chapters ahead chronicle both the rebirth of this movement and the vital, humbling lessons learned in the process. You will gain revelation on how the Lord is moving to prepare each of you for the future, including an unveiling of His glory, and a depth of purging needed to move into the higher-level God has called you to. Our prayer is that what you read will become experiential in a way that advances you and increases your capacity to understand the times. Best of all, you will grow in prayer, grow in resolve, and learn to fulfill your calling as a capable steward of the breakthroughs He longs to give you.

Because a time gate is now opening to complete the turnaround.

Speaking of which—by the grace of God, the greatest turnaround we've yet experienced actually came not to the nation or the White House, but to our own house. It answered the deepest longings of our hearts for our son and daughter. And it framed much of this new expression of the movement He is initiating in our midst.

Our Son's Christmas Miracle

In the fall of 2014, shortly after the Turnaround Verdict was first released at Faneuil Hall, our hearts became strongly resolved to pursue His national turnaround. A gentle rebuke redirected our path. Before we even sought to attain His national turnaround, the Lord wanted us to prioritize family turnarounds, according to Malachi 4:6: *"He will turn the hearts of the fathers back to their children and the hearts of the children to their fathers, so that I will not come and strike the land with complete destruction."*

The parallel verse to this is Luke 1:17. *"And it is he who will go as a forerunner before Him in the spirit and power of Elijah, to turn the hearts of fathers back to their children, and the disobedient to the attitude of the righteous, to make ready a people prepared for the Lord."*

So on Christmas Day 2014, we started a year-long project with our Lamplighter Family called "Turnaround Tuesday." Every Tuesday was set aside for contending prayer, framed at God's invitation by Daniel 7:22. Our sons and daughters collectively were being held captive by demonic ideologies, addictions, the breaking down of standards of sexuality, and so much more. We prayed fervently for our own children and for the children of those connected with us for the Lord's turnaround to prevail.

And a genuine Christmas miracle broke forth exactly one year to the day we began. For discretion's sake, I won't go into too many details. But our son, Jonathan, had fallen away from the Lord during his final few years in college. He had become so resolved in his path that he decided to break up with his college sweetheart, whom he had been dating since his final year of high school. That was a big step because he seemed hopelessly and relentlessly in love with her. But he knew his girlfriend's bond with the Lord meant everything to her, and he did not want to violate it when he resolved to follow a radically different path.

Our family had secured college for Jonathan at a Christian university, which he had chosen in part so he could pursue his relationship both with God and his girlfriend. Then things spiraled. The college introduced him to schools of philosophy which seemed to negate his faith. Students introduced him to partying. By graduation, he had disengaged both from faith in Jesus and from relationship with his bride-to-be.

As we prayed for our son and daughter, our prayers were met with God's decree. The words of Moses became the words of Jesus to their captors: LET MY CHILDREN GO!

In early December 2015, our son Jonathan contacted us. For the first time in years, he wanted to spend his birthday and Christmas together.

And on Christmas morning in 2015, again a year to the date we first began to pray, Jonathan experienced a dramatic visitation from the Lord. Jesus Himself appeared to him in a vision. With hands outstretched and open arms, the Son of God compelled our son to "return home!"

We were spending Christmas with my father in Sarasota, Florida, at the time. A knock came to our bedroom door very early Christmas morning. At least it seemed early.

"Hey, Dad, are you up?"

In a flashback to my son's childhood, my first thought was that he woke up early to open his gifts. But it soon became apparent he had much more important things on his mind. So I got up, and we talked. The conversation went something like this.

"Dad, I wanted you to be the first to know. I came home last night! Well, this morning actually."

"Came home?"

"Yeah. To Jesus! Dad, I had an encounter…"

Imagine a Christmas where your son, or your daughter, comes home to Christ! That's the best present a parent could ever receive. On the day we celebrate Christ's birth, Jesus was born anew in my son's heart and life. *"For unto us a child is born, unto us a son is given: and the government shall be upon his shoulder"* (Isa. 9:6).

But the turnarounds did not end there. A few months later Jonathan began dating his long-lost fiancée again. It took a while for trust to be reestablished. But in 2018, a beautiful wedding in Vermont launched them into the very dream they had originally pledged their lives to gain. They repaired the past to redeem the present. And they are going strong for Jesus to this day.

This same year of prayer brought incredible breakthrough for our daughter as well. We will share more on this in the next chapter. But this is just a taste of what can happen when you take hold of God's Turnaround Verdict for your children and resolve to pray relentlessly for their breakthroughs.

God is an incredibly faithful father. He is actually very sentimental. He remembers, and He leads with His heart. I promise it won't be long until your pleas are met with His decrees, in a way only He can bring forth!

Turnaround Tuesday—Now a Global Movement

In mid-June 2021 renowned prophetic leaders Lou and Therese Engle heard from a friend about our Turnaround Tuesday project, and the dramatic results. An urgent conversation followed. They both conveyed God's heart over the dire need to contend in prayer for our sons and daughters collectively in this season. It was time to start again. "This is a MOVEMENT!" he exclaimed. These words struck the core of my being.

Lightning struck again a few months later at the Global Prophetic Summit, hosted by Mike and Cindy Jacobs. I was seeking clarity for a startling vision the Lord had given in the midst of worship. I looked down, and suddenly my outstretched arms were cradling a beautiful newborn baby. Not knowing what else to do, I lifted the baby up and dedicated him to the Lord. It seemed right to share the prophetic experience with the group, a convocation of international prophets.

The hoarse, exuberant voice of Lou Engle once again brought God's clarity. "Jon—maybe that baby you saw in your vision was this Turnaround Tuesday movement!"

At Lou's request, I again recounted our son's Christmas miracle. He asked for details. And as we talked, we both became consumed again by God's heart to contend for the destiny of our children.

The next day Lou Engle was scheduled to speak. A prior message was put on hold. Instead, the prophet thundered on Turnaround Tuesday—turning the hearts of the fathers to the children and the hearts of the children to the fathers. He shared the story of Jonathan's Christmas miracle and even spoke on the Daniel 7:22 turnaround.

Jolene and I then prayed for this same miracle to be released on behalf of moms and dads on a global scale. "LET MY CHILDREN GO!"

And a new movement called Turnaround Tuesdays was globally launched as an imperative calling of the hour. Can't make this stuff up. Seriously!

Consider the story of Christ's birth. Or the "Turnaround Tuesday" project leading to my son's new birth on the morning we celebrate Christ's birth. Most of God's defining works are accomplished in the secret place. They are discovered amid everyday life, when few if any are aware of the significance of your journey. God sees. He remembers. And it's His signature to breathe on a miracle granted in the secret place and define the future by it.

Let's do this together! Like much of this book, the Turnaround Tuesday project is focused on two key goals. First, we will be praying for our sons and daughters in the spirit and natural to come fully into alignment with God's heart and destiny for them. Turnaround! Many will be contending for our moms and dads, our mentors, and friends as well. Let's see the Lord turn the hearts of the fathers to the children, and the hearts of the children back to their fathers! That's the key God identifies as the first priority in overthrowing the enemy's plan for our land.

Eliakims Arise!

Many are also praying over their regions and nations as part of this project, seeking the Lord to establish genuine fathers and mothers in seats of government and other spheres. Holy Spirit has riveted us on Isaiah 22, such a key passage for 2022 and beyond. It will prove transformative.

> Most of God's defining works are accomplished in the secret place. They are discovered amid everyday life, when few if any are aware of the significance of your journey.

"Then it will come about on that day, that I will summon My servant Eliakim the son of Hilkiah... I will hand your authority over to him, and he will become a father to the inhabitants of Jerusalem and the house of Judah. Then I will put the key of the house of David on his shoulder; when he opens, no one will shut, when he shuts, no one will open" (Isa. 22:20-22).

An evil leader was deposed. Eliakim was judged worthy and promoted over the king's domain. The key of David was conferred to him, with a commitment to carry out the covenantal legacy of his forefather. And he became the guy who made the decrees of the kingdom.

Interestingly, the name *Eliakim* means "God of arising" or "God of awakening." We are in a societal awakening right now. And the Lord wants to confer His governmental authority upon any leaders awakened by His Spirit to make a difference.

You may be among these leaders. Let's ask a question. What made Eliakim worthy? His primary qualification was laid out in a simple statement from the Lord. *"He will be a father to the house of Judah"*—the nation—*"and the inhabitants of Jerusalem"*—the capital city.

Like David before him, the great shepherd of Israel, Eliakim's qualifying attribute was simply that he carried the heart of a father into his world.

We have suffered greatly due to leaders who use their position for personal or partisan gain at the expense of the people entrusted to their care. Many godly leaders have become so focused on self-preservation that they prioritize their interests above the nation. How we need true spiritual fathers and mothers at this time. We need responsible shepherds, competent in their abilities, who lay down their lives for the sheep!

Please understand. God is in no way lacking in His capacities to release turnarounds into our world. He's not rolling around on a heavenly cloud, weighing our prayers to see if our most desperate pleas are worth responding to. He has heard our cries. He is now poised to respond. Where there may be a lack is in finding virtuous partners in Kingdom governance like Eliakim, deemed worthy to release a greater magnitude of Kingdom authority. To decree a thing and see it established.

With this at heart, isn't it wise for the Lord to offer us the opportunity to lay down our lives for the next generation through contending prayer! Turnaround Tuesday. As fathers and mothers in the spiritual realm, let's contend for the destinies of our sons and daughters. And let's pray for God's Eliakims to arise.

Equally importantly, let's seek the Lord to *become* God's Eliakims for this hour. A new breed of leaders is arising as fathers and mothers to their spheres. Like Eliakim, and David before him, they will shepherd God's people into wholeness personally and collectively. They will lead their spheres in worship, prayer, repudiation of idolatry, and covenant renewal to prepare the way of the Lord.

I want to say this prophetically: As of 2022, Eliakim becomes the standard by which the leadership of the future must be evaluated.

The Parental Revolution—a Virginia Turnaround

As of 2022, the mission has become clear. It is now time to complete the turnaround. Clearly, this Daniel 7:22 movement has now been released again from the throne, with a primary mandate to impact the sons and daughters of this generation. On both a family level and a governmental level, it's already happening.

Our home state of Virginia is proof. Against all odds, on Election Day 2021 the Virginia blues suddenly turned red. The Republican Party took credit, of course. But the fact of the matter is neither political party won this election. Instead, desperate voices of clarity—largely underestimated, marginalized, and ignored by both political parties—utterly prevailed.

Who were these mountain movers? Outraged parents!

These outraged parents simply took a stand for the well-being of their children, after enduring years of governmental impositions meant to redefine both basic morality and basic common sense. For more than a decade, truth has been sacrificed at the altar of demonic ideologies disguised as political correctness. Christianity has been marginalized. Meanwhile, the occult is openly celebrated. Godly love of country has been equated with bigotry. The innocence of our children has been consistently violated, with teachers forcing students to decide their sexual preference and gender identity as early as kindergarten.

The courageous stand of parents is now taking hold. Your prayers are fueling a parental revolution across the land! And it's only gaining momentum.

Not coincidentally, the spark that ignited the Virginia revolution was a comprehensive cover-up of a sexual assault in a local high school. School officials had implemented ordinances that allowed LGBTQ students to utilize facilities according to the gender they identified with. A young student was assaulted in her high school restroom by a biological male identifying as a transgender woman. School and government officials were involved in the cover-up. And as the case progressed, even the Biden administration got involved, requesting the Department of Justice to label many concerned parents as "domestic terrorists."

Domestic terrorists. You mean like Al Qaeda? Or the narco-terrorists now moving freely through our southern borders?

Until now most parents have largely tolerated these challenges, even at the expense of their children's innocence. But no more. I for one will unequivocally side with founding father Benjamin Franklin's observation that "rebellion to tyrants is obedience to God."

Because enough is enough. It's time to rescue our kids.

God's Turnarounds Are Always Revolutionary

God's turnarounds are always revolutionary. In fact, one of the definitions of a turnaround is a "revolution." And that's entirely appropriate. Just ponder the global shifts from the American Revolution.

You might also remember the revolutionary words of young Miriam (Mary), the mother of Jesus. While Jesus was still in her womb she prophesied, *"He brings down rulers from their thrones!"* (Luke 1:52). According to Revelation 19:11, this same Jesus executes His duties of global rulership by judging, and making war. In other words, He renders a verdict of justice—a decree—and then launches into battle to uphold, enforce, and perpetuate His decree.

Now that's revolutionary. As prophesied, we are now seeing:

- *A parental revolution,* as shared. Because again, enough is enough. American parents are taking a collective, courageous stand to secure the destinies of their children.

- *A prenatal revolution.* A major course correction is occurring now. How we steward issues of life, from the womb through old age, largely defines our legitimacy. The date 1-22-2023 will mark the 40th anniversary of Roe v. Wade. Maybe it's not a coincidence that the final draft of Turnaround Decrees was finished on 1-22-2022, after beginning to write on July 4. With an overarching intention of seeing God's mandate for LIFE nationally secured. May His turnaround decree prevail!

- *A patriot revolution.* There are unfortunate extremes. But a resurgence of a godly love of country, tied to biblical virtues which have always secured America's greatness through hours of peril, is again at hand. Just remember that to genuinely love your nation means to always pursue truth, and speak the truth.

- *A political revolution.* Can I speak plainly? Most Americans are fed up with both political parties and the divisive intolerance that they invariably impose on our nation, simply to retain their respective realms of power, wealth, and influence. It's time for a new way forward. Eliakims, arise!

- *A personal revolution.* First and foremost, it is time for your turnaround. Understanding how to partner with the Lord to

secure His dream personally is foundational for then usher-
ing His turnaround in your spheres. As you move with the
Lord, and implement the principles we are sharing, you are
guaranteed to advance in greater wholeness toward His covenant destiny for you.

Let me balance this with a statement. As a Christian and a former
journalist now in full-time ministry, truth and accuracy are nonnegotia-
ble. For this reason this book does not sugarcoat struggles, setbacks, or
the grief that sometimes encompasses the journey. When all is said and
done, the securing of God's turnaround is worth it all.

Turnaround Decree 1: Consecration for Turnaround

> *Father God, thank You for meeting me right where I am in
> my journey with You. I consecrate myself wholeheartedly to
> You and ask for a greater measure of both intimacy with You
> and authority to impact my world for Your glory. Grant me
> a spirit of wisdom and revelation in the knowledge of Jesus,
> according to Ephesians 1:17. Shape me as an Eliakim for
> my generation. Help me to pray!*
>
> *According to your Daniel 7:22 Turnaround Verdict, I ask
> that You grant me Your verdict of justice in my favor, restraining
> the forces of darkness and releasing me to possess Your Kingdom.*
>
> *And by faith right now I receive Your turnaround decrees,
> released by You to impact my life, my family, and my world.
> Help me to perceive them now and in the future. As Mir-
> iam, mother of Jesus, decreed, so I decree today: "Be it unto
> me according to Your word!"*
>
> *In Jesus' Name. Amen.*

SEVEN ON A SCROLL:
Engaging in Turnaround Tuesdays

Your faith is being activated for your turnarounds as you read. But faith without works, or corresponding action, is dead. That's why this project is a perfect companion for your journey.

Turnaround Tuesdays is an invitation for you to engage in fasting and prayer every Tuesday to secure God's turnarounds for your sons, your daughters, and your world. You can connect with us and with other believers weekly. And you can grow in your faith!

Here's how to engage:

1. Set aside time Tuesday morning, afternoon, or evening to seek God's face for your children or loved ones. Pray! And be sure to write down impressions the Lord gives you.

2. Pray Daniel 7:22. Read through the passage devotionally out loud. Gain a vocabulary corresponding to His verdict of justice in favor of yourself, your children, your loved ones.

3. Pray God's protection and blessing over your sons and daughters. Psalm 91 is a good starting point. Another amazing Scripture to decree is highlighted in chapter 2.

4. If you've received your heavenly prayer language, pray in the Spirit over your children. You don't necessarily know how to pray, but God does!

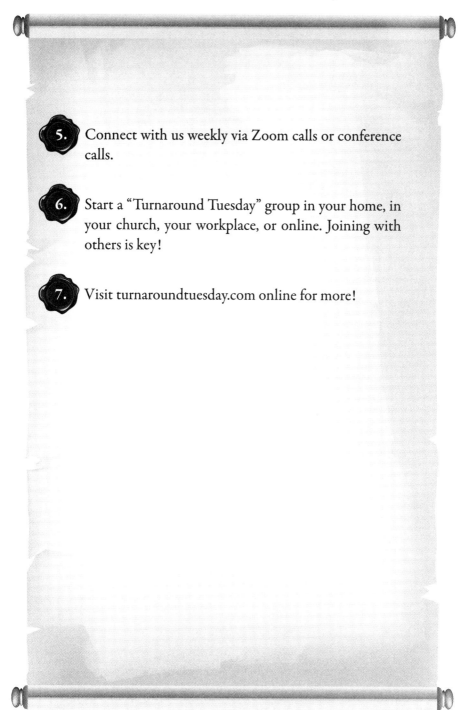

5. Connect with us weekly via Zoom calls or conference calls.

6. Start a "Turnaround Tuesday" group in your home, in your church, your workplace, or online. Joining with others is key!

7. Visit turnaroundtuesday.com online for more!

CHAPTER 2

"I WILL SAVE YOUR CHILDREN!"

"I will contend with the one who contends with you, and I will save your children!" (Isaiah 49:25).

IT WAS THE SOUND EVERY PARENT DREADS. When our daughter, Ashley, was around four years old, she slipped on stairs and fell to the bottom of the basement. Seemingly endless thumps accompanied piercing screams. I (Jon) raced down the stairs after her, praying like a madman. It was a complete surprise to find my daughter relatively calm at the foot of the stairs, seemingly barely harmed.

All at once, right in the midst of this crisis, "Isaiah 49:25" flashed through my mind. I had no idea what it said.

I immediately thought, *Lord, I'm kind of busy here, got my hands full. Could you maybe just recite to me the verse?* But that didn't happen. Instead I rushed my daughter to a local hospital just to make sure she was okay. After a thorough evaluation the doctors could not find even a fracture.

It wasn't until later that night, just before bed, that I finally found time to look up the passage. Keep in mind this incident occurred long before mobile phones or Google could provide instant results with little effort. Instead I did something that might give most of us pause today. I grabbed an actual Bible. With pages. The contents discovered were astonishing given the circumstances.

"I will contend with the one who contends with you, and I will save your children!" (Isaiah 49:25).

As I prayed, it became clear that this was more than a Scripture over a situation. It was a covenant promise from the Lord. A decree. And the Lord gave this covenantal decree to carry us through the rest of our lives.

"I will contend ... and I will save your children." From this time forward I knew God was promising to take the initiative in the healing, deliverance, and blessing of my kids. Little did I know how much more I would need this promise from the Lord later in their lives. It soon carried me, and especially my children, through challenges we could then barely even imagine. Rebellion. Discord. Demonic attacks. Damages to heart and soul were all ahead. Yet God remained utterly faithful. And again and again He has brought a turnaround where there seemed to be no way forward!

Let me be clear: Just because the Lord decrees His intervention does not mean you or I have no responsibility in the matter. Instead the opposite is true. The spiritual conflicts Jolene and I had to engage in and overcome were among the highest we have ever experienced. It actually prepared us for the many battles we were going to face nationally.

"I will contend with the one who contends with you, and I will save your children!" (Isaiah 49:25).

And honestly, if we had not had the decree promising that the Lord was going to pull our kids through, we would probably have given up long before gaining the victory.

But the other aspect of this is that *both the wars and victories belonged to the Lord, not to us.* We brought love and discipline. But like every parent, sometimes we failed. The promise that the Lord would contend, and save our children, meant that He was the one in charge of the battle. And that His pathway included mending and repairing damage we failed to prevent.

That's really difficult, especially as parents. But we realized that many times the greatest weapon of warfare was simply let go in the natural and trust Him to fulfill His promise His way.

> *"Even the captives of the mighty man will be taken away, and the prey of a tyrant will be rescued; for I will contend with the one who contends with you, and I will save your children"* (Isaiah 49:25).

When God Initiates the Decree

I believe Isaiah 49:25 is a decree from the Lord for your life and family. Consider it a sacred gift from the Father that He is initiating in your life just as He did in ours. Claim His promise! Declare His decree. I believe the covenant promise will become a foundation for your turnaround.

It's important to note that the Lord directly initiated this decree in our lives. There are 31,102 verses between the Old Testament and the New Testament. For the Lord to highlight this one, amid a moment of crisis where it was needed the most, shows His incredible watch over all of us.

Here's a question: What decrees has the Lord made personal to your life? How? What has He initiated in your life to claim, to declare, to gain? Maybe like me, a specific Scripture was highlighted to you. Maybe you've received a promise within a dream, or a prophetic word from an

outside source. These decrees are like a check in the mail to you—signed, sealed, and delivered!

Make a list of them. And then make your decrees!

Receiving and Activating Your Decrees

Receiving and applying God's turnaround decrees is actually a very simple process. The biggest key is knowing in your heart that the decree actually is sourced from God—to you personally, or to your sphere.

In basic terms, the word of the Lord is His decree over you. You must declare it to activate it. Call those things that are not as though they are! As David observed in Psalm 2, "I will announce the decree of the Lord."

I'll never forget rediscovering Christmas after I was born again. The same carols from my childhood came alive with fresh meaning and life. I was hungry to learn, especially how to hear the voice of God for myself. And God answered with a precious gift.

I heard His voice with clarity. This is what He said to me:

When you pray in the Name of Jesus, at the leading of the Holy Ghost, you are not just praying but you are prophesying, or calling those things that are not as though they are!

That's what the decree of the Lord does. It aligns the earth with His directive. Our job is to receive His decree, then declare it. The prophet Isaiah received such a commissioning:

> *"And I have put My words in your mouth and have covered you with the shadow of My hand, to establish the heavens, to found the earth, and to say to Zion, 'You are My people!'"* (Isaiah 51:16).

Seven Steps to Receive and Declare God's Decree

We'll delve more deeply into dynamics of God's decrees in the next chapter. But for now, let's look at seven easy steps to receive and declare God's decree, utilizing Isaiah 49:25 as an example. I will save your children!

1. Receive the decree of the Lord. Note that when the Lord gave me His promise to save my children, He spoke a Scripture to claim and declare. What is the Spirit of God conveying to you, either by highlighting the Word, by speaking directly by His Spirit, or both? Note the communication of Holy Spirit will NEVER violate the written Scriptures. But He will often give new revelation you have not yet perceived.

2. Write the decree! So often decrees, dreams, and other communication from Holy Spirit are lost simply because we fail to record what we've received from Him.

3. Pray in the Spirit. When possible, worship and pray in the Spirit until you sense an unction to declare the decree He has given. Most of the time it will just arise out of your spirit.

4. Declare the decree! Note the Lord put His word in Isaiah's mouth (see Isaiah 51:16). He did the same with Jeremiah (Jer. 1:10-11). By speaking the decree, you are announcing to

Receiving and applying God's turnaround decrees is actually a very simple process. The biggest key is knowing in your heart that the decree actually is sourced from God—to you personally, or to your sphere.

both the spirit realm and the earthly realm the directive of His governance. Both must yield.

5. When you decree God's word, the angelic hosts are activated. They must and will respond. Psalm 103:20 shows that the angelic hosts are activated by the VOICE of His word to perform the directive within the decree: *"Bless the Lord, you His angels, mighty in strength, who perform His word, obeying the voice of His word."* Declare the decree!

6. Train for the Turnaround! Adjust your life to gain the fulfillment of what you are seeking. This includes praying, repenting, and turning from any known sin that may give the enemy legal right to block the manifestation.

7. Keep watch over the decree. Many times a decree is not immediately manifested even after it is released. It must be "prayed through." More ahead!

These steps are essential as you partner with the Lord over your children. The promise God that will save is not a magic trump card. No decree is. Sometimes manifestations come instantaneously, other times not. But always you must keep watch in prayer. You must partner with God to birth His decree into manifestation, as He applies it to various cycles and situations of their lives.

And as you partner with the Lord both to receive and declare His decree, praying until its full manifestation, I guarantee it will carry you through many decades if you allow it to. *"I will contend with those who contend with you, and I will save your children!"*

God Is Bigger than Unforeseen Challenges

It was the moment every parent dreams of. My daughter, a new graduate from high school, sat us down to ask our perspective on plans she had made for the future. She had decided to pursue a career in the military. "Pray for me, I'm going into the Air Force," she said. Then there was a short pause followed by a flash of a smile. "No, wait. Pray for the Air Force, because I'm going into the Air Force!"

We all laughed around the table. Probably because there might have been at least a little truth in the statement. I knew just what to pray. "Lord, contend with those who contend against my daughter, in the spirit and natural! Deliver her from all harm. Mature her in You. Save our children. AND SAVE THE AIR FORCE!"

Challenges totally arose. But through it all my daughter really did well ... eventually. Ashley matured greatly through the process. She mastered new skills in a field that now has become her career. She prospered. During her time of service my daughter met and married a fantastic, highly responsible soldier who loves her wholeheartedly and treats her far better than any guy she ever dated before. They have similar interests. They are secure, stable, and hilarious together. A few years ago they even gave us a beautiful grandchild!

My point? When God promises to contend and save, He goes far beyond what we could ever imagine. This is absolutely true with both of our children.

One recent conversation brought me to tears. It went something like this.

"Dad, do you remember when we were little and you brought us to Washington, DC, and we toured the National Mall and all the memorials and I complained because I thought the mall you were bringing us to would actually have stores?"

I cringed. "Uh ... yeah, as a matter of fact I do."

"And you know how maybe I judged you for being excessively, overly patriotic ever since?"

My face turned red. I hoped she did not notice. "Well ... yeah."

"Dad, I just want you to know, after being in the Air Force I get it now. I really do. I appreciate like never before the sacrifices made to keep nation free."

That meant everything to me.

Now let me tell you a secret I've discovered. The same God who is bigger than the unforeseen challenges your children and mine will face is also bigger than the unforeseen challenges we as a nation will face.

The promise remains the same. So does the pathway through to salvation. Even the captives of the mighty will be rescued. *"I will contend with the one who contends with you. And I will save your children."*

Lessons from the Jesus Revolution

America right now stands in the balance. Our covenantal inheritance as a nation is far more vulnerable now than most leaders care to admit. We as a nation seem to be in a time similar to the 1960s, an era when new levels of sin and vileness became embraced as a cultural norm. The occult and even satanism went mainstream during the '60s. Sexual sin became celebrated, with protective purity discarded and "free love" embraced as a viable lifestyle. Countless marriages and families were destroyed. Fathers fled. Mothers fled. Children often became the most impacted, infusing despondency, hopelessness, and anger into their hearts. All the while extreme drug use mesmerized the masses and thwarted the true potential of countless individuals.

And a generation who previously considered Judeo-Christian values normative found themselves suddenly at the end of the road.

It was during this tumultuous time that God broke in with a Jesus revolution. A massive tsunami of evangelism swept multitudes into the Kingdom. California coasts especially were filled with baptism services. New wineskins such as Calvary Chapel and the Vineyard movement sprang up. Revelation on spiritual warfare, on apostolic and prophetic ministry, expanded our horizons. Instantaneous healings and deliverances became normative. And Billy Graham filled stadiums as a nation turned to Jesus.

He did it then. Can He do it now? The Lord is looking for forerunners who dare to dream with Him for a dramatic recovery of revival. A new Jesus revolution. It's in our blood. It's part of America's DNA. We are a nation of awakening!

The greater question to ask is, What sparked this Jesus revolution? Preeminently, a massive wave of desperate prayer just beforehand. Fathers and mothers, grandfathers and grandmothers, teachers and leaders fell to their faces and engaged with God over their children. Their intercession forged a Glory pathway for revival to sweep the land.

And it's about to happen again. You can feel it in the atmosphere. A new grace of birthing prayer is being released for the deliverance of this generation. LET MY CHILDREN GO!

Decreeing and Receiving—the Process

When God initiates a project, He decrees the end from the beginning. *"I am God, and there is no one like Me, declaring the end from the beginning and from ancient times things which have not been done, saying, 'My plan will be established!'"* (Isa. 46:9-10).

Many times the manifestation of God's decrees seem almost spontaneous, in real time. Other times the process may seem extended. But in all cases there is a process. Understanding the process helps you to better partner with the Lord through it.

God's decree initiates the process, frames the results, and announces the arrival in its proper timing. But you have to know your partnership is vital to bring it to pass.

> America right now stands in the balance. Our covenantal inheritance as a nation is far more vulnerable now than most leaders care to admit.

In that context it's kind of like having a baby. Especially when contending for the salvation of your children or loved ones to turn to the Lord. No wonder Jesus called it a born-again experience!

First, there's a conception. Then comes hidden growth. On the surface it appears nothing is going on. In reality, every facet of your baby, your answer to prayer, is in development. Then comes the discovery that a miracle is on its way! The beautiful miracle inside is worth living for, even radically changing your lifestyle to prepare the way for.

But it's not easy. No wonder carrying a prayer project has many times been referred to as "carrying a prayer burden."

Now the old-timers had enough sense to pray these burdens through to breakthrough. For some reason many in our generation have let go of this lost art. Decrees alone don't always finish the job. Heed their wisdom and pray through!

That's when there is a birthing. It's time! Often the arrival of God's promise is accompanied by breakthrough declarations. Sometimes it involves intense "birthing prayer" often referred to as travail.

Travail as a Weapon of War

Recently the Lord really focused Jolene and me on Psalm 6, where "the voice of our tears" is met by God's movement of breakthrough and vindication. One of the key verses He gave us was Isaiah 42:14. *"Now like a woman in labor (travail) I will groan, I will gasp and pant and lay waste the mountains."*

As a guy, I've mostly paid attention to the verse before. It's actually how I picture His collaboration with us. *"The Lord marches forth like a warrior, He rouses His zeal like a man of war; He will utterly prevail against His enemies!"* (verse 13). This passage awakens fire in me every time. I want to join with the Lord to utterly, completely prevail against His enemies, don't you? I want our procession to be so directed by the Lord that He is marching forth in our midst as the conquering king!

And if there's anything I know about the season, it's that the Lord is raising His war cry for battle right now. His zeal is aroused!

But how He wars in this season is very telling. One facet of His warfare is actually compared to *a woman in travail,* bringing to birth His purposes. All that said, travailing prayer is a major weapon of warfare. And it is key to gain His new birth of freedom!

And it is an absolute sign of apostolic fathering and mothering. The greatest apostle in the New Testament described it this way: *"My children, with whom I am again in labor until Christ is formed in you..."* (Gal. 4:19).

So how do you enter into this dimension of prayer? First and foremost, by praying in the Spirit. When you pray in the Spirit you allow Holy Spirit to intercede through you the precise plans and purposes of the Father. Further, He partners with you to bring to birth His desire. *"'Not by might nor by power, but by My Spirit,' says the Lord"* (Zech. 4:6)!

> *"For we know that the whole creation groans and suffers the pains of childbirth together. ... Now in the same way the Spirit also helps our weakness; for we do not know what to pray for as we should, but the Spirit Himself intercedes for us with groanings too deep for words; and He who searches*

the hearts knows what the mind of the Spirit is, because He intercedes for the saints according to the will of God" (Romans 8:22, 26-27).

Beyond the End of the Road

Alaska, as a breakthrough state, has been highlighted to us in this season. As you will discover in chapter 6, the Lord mandated Alaska to release a Daniel 7:22 decree that defines the turnaround movement of today, so similar to the Jesus revolution of the 1960s and '70s.

One afternoon we boarded a ferry from the town of Homer. A coastal town on the Kenai peninsula, Homer is known as "the end of the road." There's a very legitimate reason. Homer, Alaska, is the westernmost destination of the entire US highway system. It actually is THE END of the road!

Maybe you've been there before? Not Homer per se. But maybe your own end of the road?

It happens a lot in the midst of everyday life. It always happens during childbirth! And also when you are bringing to birth the purposes of the Lord. There comes a point when your strongest efforts and noblest intentions still can't get the job done. Your options seem gone, and though you know what God wants you simply see no way to bring it to pass.

Okay... I see you've got a T-shirt from Homer too.

Opening your heart to God during these situations will always secure His assistance. Talk with Him as you would to a friend. Be honest with Him. You'll soon find something deep within you summoning you to arise. To pray. To decree. To take the right steps and advance His way. In process—this is a word from the Lord to you—*the end of the road will become a gateway to your new beginnings.*

And you'll leave behind a trail of broken-down barriers which once defined your limitations. Decree this now!

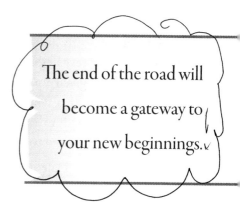

The end of the road will become a gateway to your new beginnings.

Fair warning here for those who aspire to become forerunners. You will always want to know what's beyond the end of the road. Which is why, in Homer, we boarded a boat with the Alaskan wilderness as our destination.

Besides our team there were maybe 20 passengers at best when the ferry left the dock. Which made conversations easy to hear. Someone on the other side of the boat started talking about Jesus, and it caught my attention. To my utter surprise I found myself speaking with an older apostolic evangelist who had travelled eight million miles around the world ministering the Gospel.

And in the late 1960s, he unexpectedly became a father of the Jesus revolution.

Now what are the chances, leaving "the end of the road" on a ferry with 20 passengers to an island wilderness in Alaska, that a father of the Jesus Movement would also be on board? My spirit stood at attention, for all the right reasons.

Dale Van Steenis told us the story of how he witnessed the spark of the Jesus Movement firsthand. He was coaching a pastor in Southern California who had given up all hope after his church split for the third time. While with them he attended a weekly prayer meeting at the church, which the pastor had facilitated for almost a decade. At one time the prayer meeting was packed. But now only a few die-hards showed up.

Die-hards mostly anyway. Of course the discreet prayers of the pastor would have revealed he was actually seeking the Lord to move on. He had all but given up. But the other consistent participant was an 84-year-old grandma who wept and travailed continually in groaning prayer, contending for the church, for lost sons and daughters, and anyone else who happened to come to mind.

Not long after Dale attended this prayer gathering, a hippie in a Speedo, strung out on drugs and alcohol, came into a sparsely attended Sunday night meeting. He became so disruptive the pastor almost threw him out. Amazingly, he let him stay. And long story short, the hippie got radically saved and delivered.

Not long after, the young man—no longer in a Speedo—asked the pastor if he would hold a special meeting on Monday evening, just for him and a few friends. Accommodations were reluctantly made for the extra service.

Turns out the hippie Speedo guy was extremely influential in Hollywood. The pastor had no idea. That Monday approximately a thousand of the man's closest friends attended the service! All ended up getting rocked for Jesus. And according to this apostolic evangelist taking a ferry from the end of the road into the Alaskan wilderness, who caught my ear by mentioning Jesus, that meeting became a spark for the entire Jesus revolution!

I want to see that spark released today, don't you? We are all contending. In many ways it may feel like you're at the end of the road. But a new Jesus revolution is just beyond! You and I are going to mark our children for the Lord, laying tracks in prayer for their turnaround.

And as this movement grows, an entire generation is going to meet the Lord at the threshold. It's turnaround time.

"Even the captives of the mighty man will be taken away,
and the prey of a tyrant will be rescued; for I will contend

with the one who contends with you, and I will save your children" (Isa. 49:25).

Turnaround Decree 2: "I Will Save Your Children"

"Even the captives of the mighty man will be taken away, and the prey of a tyrant will be rescued; for I will contend with the one who contends with you, and I will save your children" (Isa. 49:25).

Father God, I am in awe of Your thoughtful, watchful care over me and my family, including the family of my future. in Your presence I now receive an aspect of Your Daniel 7:22 turnaround verdict in my favor. "I will save your children!"

I receive Isaiah 49:25 now as Your decree over my life. Accordingly I decree that You now contend with the forces in the spiritual realm and the natural realm who contend with me. And that You now rescue My children from their grasp.

Father God, I dedicate my children—present and future—to You, entrusting them into Your care. I call them out to You by name (do this now). Father God, I also dedicate my bloodline, my entire family tree, to You alone. Please grant the annulment of all pacts and dedications made with spiritual entities, as I have decided they must be owned by the Lord Jesus Christ alone. I ask that all legal claims made by these entities to own, influence, or harm my children now be annulled by the body and blood of Jesus Christ.

According to Your decree I declare my children now enter into complete freedom from their grasp. The captives of the mighty tyrants are now rescued! And this deliverance by the Lord Jesus Christ now manifests in every aspect of their lives. Lord, I decree that the end of the road now becomes a gateway to our new beginnings!

Lord, I thank You that You judge and make war. You render Your decree and make war to uphold and enforce it in the earth. Accordingly, I thank You for now making war to free my children! I call them fully back to You and fully free to fulfill their covenant destiny, in Jesus' Name!

SEVEN ON A SCROLL:
Receiving and Declaring Your Decree

1. Receive the decree of the Lord. What is the Spirit of God conveying to you, either by His Word, by His Spirit, or both?

2. Write the decree! So often decrees, dreams, and other communication from Holy Spirit are lost simply because we fail to record what we've received from Him.

3. Pray in the Spirit. When possible, worship and pray in the Spirit until you sense an unction to declare the decree He has given you.

4. Declare the decree! By speaking the decree, you are announcing to both the spirit realm and the earthly realm the directive of His governance.

5. Activate the angelic hosts. When you decree God's word, the angelic hosts are activated (see Psalm 103:20).

6. Train for the Turnaround! This includes praying, repenting, and turning from any known sin that may give the enemy legal right to block the manifestation.

7. Keep watch over your decree. It must be "prayed through"!

CHAPTER 3

SCROLLS OF YOUR KINGSHIP

"You have made them to be kings and priests to our God, and they will reign upon the earth!" (Revelation 5:10).

IT WASN'T SUPPOSED TO HAPPEN THIS WAY. The apostle John, beloved Jewish disciple who leaned his head on Jesus and gained His private counsel, probably should have been influencing the world from a palace on Zion. He was capable of it. Or at least he was capable of a preaching, writing, and ministry career poised to change the world.

So often that pathway seemed firm—only to suffer persecution, crushing betrayals, and even attempts on his life. Then came exile. What crime deserves this punishment—writing that God is love? Declaring to Jew and Gentile that you must be born again?

Not that a house on God's hill was actually attainable in this midnight hour. Through the reign of Pax Romana, the palaces of Zion and even God's holy Temple were now smoldering ruins, their treasures plundered. Christians in Rome confirmed that the Temple menorah had in fact been stolen by the global governmental superpower. It was put on display in an audacious victory parade, carried through city gates on the humiliated shoulders of Jewish resistance fighters.

Generations before, a resistance fighter named Judah Maccabee had relit this very menorah to reconsecrate the Temple after his band of spiritual revolutionaries overtook a similar occupation. But the resistance army of John's generation had instead been brutally crushed. Perhaps a sign from the Lord that the Covenant People had once again failed to fully turn. In a very real way, their lamp had been extinguished.

The Roman Empire expressed to the world a benign façade. But in its depths, there was a viciousness that could only be sourced in idolatry. John had watched the Roman weapon of torture raised to its most horrifying heights over Zion, with the very Son of God nailed to its wood.

Jesus rose, of course. But Zion fell. Jews were scattered to the four corners of the earth. Israel was no more. Though John prayed fervently for a turnaround, it seemed impossible. Now even the covenant nation would have to be born again.

Such were the days in which he lived.

Instead of a palace on Zion, the great apostle's living quarters consisted of a small cave in a large mountain on a barren, nearly deserted island in the Aegean Sea where the Romans hosted a small prison colony. The island was called Patmos.

When John was young, he often dreamed of the romantic encounters gained in such a cave as pictured in the Song of Songs 2:14: "*My dove in the clefts of the rock, in the hiding places on the mountainside, show me your face, let me hear your voice; for your voice is sweet, and your face is lovely*" (NIV).

These adolescent longings from long ago now seemed almost prophetic. Given John's lifestyle, romance had proven elusive. But encounters? That was another matter altogether.

For it was in this literal cleft in the rock, midway up a steep mountain pathway, that John heard the voice of his longtime Friend. He saw His face. He experienced His eternal throne. Then he recorded these epic cave encounters in a book called the Apocalypse. Or, in English, the book of Revelation.

Distribution of these scrolls had been difficult, given John's isolation. But even in hiding, his team managed to get the word out. Seven copies were delivered to the seven churches to whom the word of the Lord was given. With a personal scroll kept in reserve.

Perhaps it was only appropriate that the King of Glory would reveal His glory from within a cave. His friend Jesus had been born in such a cave. That was where He was wrapped by His parents in swaddling clothes. Now the gentle Healer, the slain Lamb, appeared to the apostle John as the very Lion of Judah—the Commander of Armies Himself. Clothed in a robe dipped in blood, vanquishing His enemies, judging, and making war to bring justice to the martyrs, to the nations, and to His beloved Israel.

Jesus' mother, Miriam, had always said He was born to bring down unjust rulers from their thrones. For obvious reasons, Rome considered the very words seditious. Miriam was labeled a domestic terrorist. Peter and Paul had joined the ranks of Roman martyrs. Lord Jesus, it is high time this dimension of Your calling became fulfilled!

One encounter John especially treasured. In the Spirit on the Lord's day, John saw the throne, with God the Father seated upon it. Scrolls were in His right hand. John knew intuitively the scroll framed out humanity's redemption. Opening it would release God's intended intervention on the earth.

How much this was needed. Yet the scrolls remained sealed.

"I saw in the right hand of Him who sat on the throne a scroll written inside and on the back, sealed up with seven seals. And I saw a strong angel proclaiming with a loud voice, "Who is worthy to open the scroll and to break its seals?" And no one in heaven or on the earth or under the earth was able to open the scroll or to look into it. Then I began to weep greatly because no one was found worthy to open the scroll or to look into it..." (Revelation 5:1-4).

Unexpectedly the sight provoked within John a deep groaning. Heaven was paradise. There were supposed to be no tears. Yet John found himself weeping because no one in Heaven or earth had been found worthy to open these scrolls of mankind's redemption, or even peer into their contents.

On earth, the experience was called travail. He found himself travailing for the release of the scrolls.

That's when a voice interrupted him. "Stop weeping!" The man commanded, with a blunt kindness that seemed distinctly Jewish. John turned and perceived an elder with great authority conferred by God to rule. He was young, yet ancient.

> *"Stop weeping; behold, the Lion that is from the tribe of Judah, the Root of David, has overcome so as to be able to open the scroll and its seven seals!"* (Rev. 5:5).

John looked, and a Lamb appeared, slain yet standing. A Lamb, yet a Lion. He came and took the scroll out of the right hand of Him who sat on the throne. Immediately the heavenly creatures and the elders, twenty-four in all, fell prostrate before the Son of God.

> *When He had taken the scroll, the four living creatures and the twenty-four elders fell down before the Lamb, each one holding a harp and golden bowls full of incense, which are the prayers of the saints. And they sang a new song, saying, "Worthy are You to take the scroll and to break its seals; for You were slaughtered, and You purchased people for God with Your blood from every tribe, language, people, and nation. You have made them to be kings and priests to our God, and they will reign upon the earth!"* (Revelation 5:8-10).

Travail for the Release of the Scrolls

How deeply do you long for a turnaround? If John wept over the release of these "turnaround decrees" even from Heaven, how much more should we?

Again, to a large extent travailing prayer is still needed for the "birthing" of these scrolls in the earth. John's experience gives us a tremendous pattern. First, it is vital to enter into throne room transactions for your turnaround, gaining revelation of His decree. In this chapter you will gain keys for this. We then enter into prayer by the Spirit for breakthrough, following His directives until His decree manifests on earth. Signs may or may not immediately accompany. But in your spirit you will know it's accomplished, and your pleas are being met with His decree.

Covenant Unlocks Turnaround

In response to John's travail, the great apostle sees the risen Christ—the Lamb standing, the Lion of Judah—as He is granted dominion by the Father to unseal the scrolls of mankind's redemption. Note again the pattern. Times of intensive intercession for others often become doorways to a greater revelation of Jesus.

The elders and living creatures before the throne proclaim Jesus' worthiness to take the scroll based on His unimaginable investment to redeem you and me. He took upon Himself the punishment for the sins of all mankind, to make His redemption available to all.

These scenes portray how the covenant Jesus made through His own body and blood had been evaluated and validated by the exacting standards of Heaven's Court. The verdict came for our redemption. Judgment was rendered in favor of the saints!

Now every judgment rendered and every decree issued is based upon this legal precedent of Messiah's redemption, secured by covenant through His own body and blood.

Whether your turnaround is a healing, a breakthrough of provision, or an exodus movement for an entire nation, covenant with God then becomes the legal foundation for both the turnarounds He sets in motion, and the decrees which define these turnarounds. Covenant is the key that unlocks Heaven's scrolls of destiny.

Scrolls of Your Kingship

Just before the 2020 elections the Lord gave me a prophetic experience directly related to this, where He showed me a release of His scrolls of redemption for America. We'll close out the chapter with this encounter. But for now, let's focus on the decree made by the elders and living creatures as the scrolls were released from the Father's hand:

> *"You purchased people for God with Your blood from every tribe, language, people, and nation. You have made them to be kings and priests to our God, and they will reign upon the earth!"*

As recorded on this scroll, when you gave your life to Jesus, your eternal destiny was sealed through the body and blood of Jesus. You have been redeemed to God! Your name is recorded in the Book of Life. You are eternally a citizen of Heaven.

But friends, there is an aspect of your redemption that God expects you to fulfill right here on earth. Through Christ's redemption you have been made a priest to the Lord. You have also been made a king. And according to this decree, you will reign upon the earth!

The Bible says that you have become seated with Christ *"in heavenly places"* (Eph. 2:6 KJV). Ponder this for a moment. Whether you were born in a mansion or a cave, you have been born again into a throne of authority that ultimately surpasses every king in the earth!

You have become royalty. Literally born of royal blood.

Note that this throne of authority was conferred the moment you were born again. Both in the spiritual realm and the natural world, thrones are established by covenant. You gained a seat before God's throne the moment you entered into covenant with Him. And it is this covenant which determines both your ultimate legitimacy and your ultimate authority.

I cannot emphasize enough the importance of this precept. It has the potential to dramatically impact the course of your life.

And it has the potential to direct the course of the nation. Our founders entered into covenant with God. This covenant has been wholeheartedly renewed from generation to generation, including now. Follow this with me. Covenants establish thrones of governance. Therefore the thrones of governance of this nation belong to God.

Your Pleas, God's Decree

How do you reign from this throne? Actually, the very same way by which other kings exercise their rulership—by making decrees. As shown in chapter 2, the first step is always to seek the Lord until His decree becomes clear. Following the example of the apostle John, enter in to the presence of the Holy Spirit. Declare your position before God's throne, seated with Christ in heavenly places. In Jesus' Name, take your seat! And receive His directive.

The Bible says, *"If we ask anything according to His will, He hears us. And if we know that He hears us in whatever we ask, we know that we*

...there is an aspect of your redemption that God expects you to fulfill right here on earth. Through Christ's redemption you have been made a priest to the Lord. You have also been made a king. And according to this decree, you will reign upon the earth!

have the requests which we have asked from Him" (1 John 5:14-15). In every God-ordained prayer project, there comes a moment when what you've contended for comes to pass.

Sometimes it is immediate. But as mentioned, in bigger projects especially, there is often a time of contending for these scrolls to be released. John wept. The prophet Daniel fasted and prayed for 21 days until the angel of the Lord broke through, and Heaven's message was delivered. Many times, throne room decrees become revealed only as our prayer project comes to completion. The Lord may even direct you to a specific place at a specific time to declare His breakthrough word.

Securing God's turnaround often requires intentionality that sometimes even transcends time. Watch though—there is great blessing in the process! Even as you read this, the anguish many of you have suffered in previous seasons is finally giving way. You will see with new eyes how the Lord is now moving to protect you even while building you up. Most importantly, you are being freed to grow in greater intimacy with the Lord. That's the most precious turnaround for all of us!

It's important to note the challenges you are facing are first inherently spiritual. Neither political dominance, economic dominance, media dominance, or religious dominance carries the power to prevail. Only the supernatural power unleashed by God's intervention in our midst can restrain evil and genuinely secure His turnaround.

And that power, my friend, is again first accessed through prayer. The good news is, as you and I make our appeal to Heaven, the Lord stands ready to respond. *Your plea will be met with His decree!*

Keys to Aligning for Breakthrough

God has ordained that you rule with Him as a king and priest over your spheres. Again, this rulership is largely accomplished through praying, then making decrees that are carried out in the spiritual and natural realms.

As the psalmist said, *"I will announce the decree of the Lord!"* (Ps. 2:7).

In our own ministry, receiving immediate, substantive, longstanding breakthroughs through the release of God's decrees is now by far the norm. It is our most consistent pattern of results. Why? Because primarily, receiving consistent breakthroughs is a matter of gaining proper alignment with God's throne. Then these breakthroughs have free course.

Here are seven factors to consider.

1. **Is the decree God's will or presumption?** When we experience a delay, the first question is always whether or not we are fully in alignment with God's revealed will—by His Spirit and by His word—or simply operating in presumption. This is such a key question. Because decreeing out of personal desire or presumption can actually be equated to witchcraft.

2. **Timing.** Is our expectation properly aligned with God's timing? For instance, Isaiah decreed the birth of Israel's Messiah, but the manifestation of this miracle was actually some seven

hundred years away. When seeking God's turnaround, it's important to perceive where you are in the birthing process.

3. **Legal access to restrain.** It is vital to explore with the Lord where the enemy may have gained legal standing to withhold a breakthrough the Lord intends to grant. Breaches of covenant through sin—especially the sin of idolatry, either presently or generationally—are by far the primary blockages. Which is why it is so vital to learn how to partner with God to repair the past, so we can unlock His best for our present and future. We will explore this more in chapter 8.

4. **Go to the root.** *"If the root is holy, so are the branches"* (Rom. 11:16). Sometimes you have to deal with issues the way a surgeon deals with skin cancer. You must pull back the layers until the true root is exposed. Then things shift!

5. **Check your giving.** Alignment with God's directive regarding the divine exchange of tithes and offerings, as recorded in Malachi 4, is not an option—at least if you want the heavens to open and the devourer be rebuked.

6. **Authority to decree.** A fifth factor to consider is a person's standing before the Lord to make the decree. As with any governmental structure there is authority in the Kingdom. Genuine turnaround decrees are sourced from the throne of God, and stewarded through His appointed authorities. Of course, God's appointees are often different from man's. Just look at David! As a shepherd boy, he took down the giant that had paralyzed both the king and his top warriors.

7. **Apostolic alignment.** My counsel for everybody is to move with what God has put on your heart, collaborating with godly mentors and allowing His dream to mature in you through the process. Believe in yourself. Believe in the godly mentors the Lord has placed in your path to help you

Scrolls of Your Kingship

advance. And believe in the sacredness of what God has deposited in your heart!

Dynamics of God's Decrees

"And thou shalt also decree a thing and it shall be established unto thee. And the light shall shine upon thy ways" (Job 22:28 KJV).

Let's explore a few dynamics related to decrees. A decree is more than a strong declaration spoken with enough volume and confidence to make it seem believable to those listening. Been there, done that, bought the tee shirt many times myself! Yet most often, the results simply failed to fully materialize.

Decrees are actually issued from two classifications of authorities—either from appointed governors such as kings, presidents, and lawgivers, or from judges via courtroom verdicts. The stewards of God's Kingdom decrees must in the same manner be cultivated, appointed, and validated by God.

Again, I'm not trying to disqualify you here. Instead, you're going to discover in these pages the extraordinary lengths God Himself has gone to qualify you to attain this authority, functioning as a king and priest before Him.

> Governmental authority is both conferred and earned. You have a crown to gain, and a throne of rulership to steward.

But it's vital to understand this governmental authority is both conferred and earned. You have a crown to gain, and a throne of rulership to steward. And as in every other expression of increase in God's Kingdom, you have been afforded the potential to gain in earned authority as a governor of His decrees.

Decrees—Sourced in Courtroom Verdicts

Whatever branch of government decrees are issued from, to be considered legitimate they must always be validated by a court of law.

And in the judicial system, a primary definition of a decree is actually an order handed down by a judge that resolves the issues in a court case.[1] In other words, decrees become the medium by which courtroom verdicts are administrated. When the judge issues his verdict, decrees are stipulated that administrate the verdict as it applies to each party and situation involved. Marriage certificates and divorce decrees are two of the most common examples of this.

So—this is very important—decrees are sourced from verdicts or legal judgments. Even the Daniel 7:22 Turnaround Verdict is sourced from a higher verdict, one Jesus invested His own body and blood to attain for you and me. Our redemption! This is the ultimate expression of judgment in favor of the saints, restraining the enemy and releasing the saints to possess the Kingdom.

Decrees Administer Verdicts Generationally

And at the discretion of Heaven's Court, from this one turnaround verdict will come many turnaround decrees as applicable to each party involved, even through successive generations. Including yours.

As an example to learn from, let's return to Esther's decree. It is actually sourced in the throne room experience from which Daniel recorded the turnaround verdict.

Prior to Esther's ascension into rulership, she and her people were under an existential threat. The Jews had been forced into exile in ancient Persia, now modern-day Iran.

Similar to Iran today, anti-Semitism raged within the halls of government. And Haman, an ancient prototype of Adolf Hitler, had planned a holocaust.

Esther led her people in fasting. She then stood before both her king and Her King, pleading her case. Judgment was rendered in her favor. Thanks to Esther's unprecedented intervention, instead of succumbing to death the Jewish people were protected and preserved, even granted the right to bear arms for self-protection. Further, they even gained permission to return to Israel. Literally to possess the Kingdom!

Through the ordeal, Esther was promoted into rulership with her king and husband. Even to rule half the Kingdom! Further, she was given authority to write a decree that the national government from region to region was obligated to obey!

Now that's a turnaround. Revolutionary!

Esther's story played out just as Daniel had prophesied one generation before. Judgment was literally rendered in favor of the saints, restraining the enemy, and releasing the saints to possess the Kingdom. Again, Esther's turnaround was predicated on the verdict from Heaven prophesied by the prophet Daniel. Yet she may not have even known about it when the circumstances played out Just as Daniel prophesied!

Never forget this. The Lord remembers. When He renders judgment on a matter, He is personally obligated to fulfill it—even through ensuing generations.

Let me say prophetically there are countless scrolls for this present hour, many of which have been pioneered by our forefathers and all predicated on the Daniel 7:22 Turnaround Verdict, that must be decreed and released in order for their intended fulfillment to be activated in our time. And as with Esther, this invitation is being extended to you.

"He Judges and Makes War"

This brings us to perhaps the most important part of the chapter. Because no government functions without the capacity to enforce the decrees that are made. Jesus as the Lamb of God became the sacrifice whose death secured our verdict of redemption. Jesus as the Lion of Judah, risen from the grave, both stewards this verdict and makes war to uphold and enforce it. He has attained all authority to rule all realms of the heavens and earth!

Consider Revelation 19:11-14 with me:

> "And I saw heaven opened, and behold, a white horse, and He who sat on it is called Faithful and True, and in righteousness **He judges and makes war**... He is clothed with a robe dipped in blood, and His name is called The Word of God. And the armies which are in heaven, clothed in fine linen, white and clean, were following Him on white horses."

On a case-by-case basis, Jesus renders a verdict of justice for His people. Then He makes war to uphold and enforce this verdict in the earth. This facet of the King's majesty is being unveiled to a much greater measure. He is the Lord of Hosts!

As recorded in Revelation 19, the apostle John saw a picture of this. Jesus is moving between Heaven and earth to dislodge antichrist forces attempting to enslave humanity. He is returning to Zion to take His rightful throne. And the armies of Heaven are following Him, poised for the greatest battle mankind will ever witness.

Here's an unsettling fact. Many want to follow Jesus to the throne, but far fewer want to follow Him into battle. Mostly because this aspect of your calling involves investment. It involves training. It involves sacrifice.

But no battle on earth is won without it.

The Lord is raising up His army. Gideon forces are now in training to overcome! And you and I are hereby summoned to take our places. I say, let's roll!

Vision—Lion of Judah Roaring Over Nation

Two weeks before the 2020 elections, I was in Oklahoma City for the annual HAPN prayer conference when the Lord gave me a vision conveying how He is redeeming scrolls of destiny, even for our nation. A form materialized before my eyes. I knew immediately this was the Lion of Judah. At first His appearance was translucent. As I continued to watch, His appearance increased in vibrancy and glory. Then this Lion began to roar over the nation. The manifest presence of God accompanied the visitation.

In the midst of the vision, times and seasons began to become clear. I saw how the season we were entering was similar to the midnight hour when Jacob wrestled with the Angel of the Lord. Eventually at dawn he prevailed. Until that time darkness obscured both the form of the Lord and the surroundings of his environment. They were barely able to be perceived.

And a word from the Lord then came.

It has seemed to you that a veil of darkness has been restricting your full capacity to perceive and understand. As you now engage with the Lord, the dawn begins to awaken. Your wrestling leads to breakthrough. This veil of darkness that has obscured both your perception of Jesus and your understanding of the times IS BEING REMOVED.

Remember, names convey identity. Just as Jacob became Israel, many of you are even going to be given a new name from the Lord prophetically. The Hebrew meaning of Jacob is "Deceiver." The name given to him by the angel was "Israel," meaning "Prince of God" or "one who wrestles with God." Only after this blessing was bestowed was he allowed to cross over, entering the land of Israel as Israel.

It is the same with you. It is the same with our nation. Deception must and will be left on the other side of the river. As you enter into your new commissioning as a king and priest, you become legitimized, authorized, and anointed to possess your portion of God's inheritance in your nation. It will take a war!

In the midst of this appearance of the Lion of Judah, the Lord began to show me great turmoil coming in the 2020 elections and beyond. I saw and prophesied on record that the elections would be contested. I also saw how travailing prayer and fasting needed to continue at least through November 11, the 400th anniversary of the Mayflower Compact. It was as though, in the end, only covenant with God would have the power to settle the coming conflict over our land.

The Lion Releases the Scrolls

As you already know, in the entire Bible there is only one direct reference to Jesus as the Lion of the Tribe of Judah, and that is found in Revelation 5. The Lion releases the scrolls. In this passage He is revealed both as the slain Lamb and the Lion of Judah. Victorious in His resurrection after paying the price for our sin, He has been granted the authority to steward the scroll of God's redemption.

By the Spirit of revelation I saw how, in conjunction with Jesus' redemption and our combined intercession, *the scroll of the Father's intended destiny for our nation had been redeemed.* And the Lord is roaring His enforcement over our land!

Beloved, it's turnaround time.

Remember, this vision of the Lion of Judah was given just two weeks before the 2020 elections. Given the timing I initially figured the elections were going to ensure a second term for President Trump. But when I prayed, in my spirit I sensed anything but this assurance.

Beware again of presumption. Friends, I've learned this the hard way. In all things we need to rely on Holy Spirit instead of our own understanding. The vision I initially interpreted as an indication of an election victory was actually given as a stabilizing anchor through a very difficult season spurred by very different results. And through it I discovered that God's agenda to advance His Kingdom is often radically different from our own.

Scrolls from Heaven are being unfurled and released, bringing extraordinary shaking and exposure. His turnaround decrees are now being roared across the spectrum for you, for your children, for the Body of Christ, for Israel and America, and for many nations of the earth. A window to a new era is opening. This book is written to educate and equip you to maximize your opportunity. And in a way not unlike Esther or our nation's founders, you are now invited to partner with Jesus Himself to define this new way forward.

Let's now enter the storm of the 2020 elections and their aftermath. You will gain a prophetic perspective on the unimaginable challenges at hand as well as God's promise for national turnaround. The supernatural way in which this decree was given will astound you.

All that said, we begin our journey at the White House, just one day before the defining incident now known as the "Capitol Storm."

Turnaround Decree 3: Lion of Judah

> *Father God, in Jesus' Name I thank You now for Throne Room revelation to see Jesus as both the slain Lamb and the resurrected Lion. The scrolls of my redemption are in Your hands! Thank You for giving me eyes to see, ears to hear, and a heart to understand Your will and Your ways. Roar Your covenant destiny over me and over my world!*
>
> *Thank You, Lord, that by Your body and blood You have redeemed both my life and my destiny. You have made me to be a king and a priest. Lord, I receive Your coronation. I am royalty! I receive Your commissioning. I am a priest before Your Throne! Help me to grow in this newfound identity You have bestowed upon me. Help me to understand how to reign in the earth for Your glory!*
>
> *Lord, I decree You are now granting me Throne Room vision. Synergize me with Your Throne and the activity of Your Throne. Lord, I decree my times are in Your hands! Rebuke the devourer of time and align me with Your Throne Room timing. Make me a Throne Room watchman!*
>
> *Father, Your Word declares that "in Your book were written all the days that were ordained for me, when as yet there was not one of them" (Ps. 139:16). Make the scrolls of Your redemption over my life very real to me. Help me to perceive them. Align me with Your turnaround decrees!*
>
> *Lord, I invite the dominion of the Lion of Judah in my life and spheres. I decree that You now align my life with*

Your turnaround decrees. Align my family, my church, my work, my nation.

Your Word declares that **"He who began a good work among you will complete it by the day of Christ Jesus"** *(Phil. 1:6). Please complete the turnaround that You have begun in my life. Healing. Wholeness. Provision. Strength! Shalom and love in my marriage and family. Turnarounds for my children. Deliverance from the hand of the enemy!*

Lord, as you worked with Jacob, I decree that You are now bringing me through Your refining process to gain the fullness of promises You desire to release—to me and through me to Your people. Lord, I decree Your breakthrough, and I receive Your breakthroughs in the spiritual realm and over my circumstances. Anywhere I'm stuck, get me unstuck. Pull me across the threshold into Your new season!

As with Jacob and as with Israel, before Your Throne I now lay claim to Your covenant destiny and Your inheritance for my life, in Jesus' Name. Now complete the turnaround! Release the fullness of Your redemptive purpose and destiny, in Jesus' Name.

Turnaround Decree 3

SEVEN ON A SCROLL:
Aligning for Breakthrough

1. Is the decree God's will or presumption? When we experience a delay, the first question is always whether or not we are fully in alignment with God's revealed will.

2. Timing is also an issue. Is our expectation properly aligned with God's timing?

3. Legal access to restrain. It is vital to explore with the Lord where the enemy may have gained any legal standing to withhold a breakthrough the Lord intends to grant.

4. Go to the root. *"If the root is holy, so are the branches"* (Rom. 11:16).

5. Check your giving. Alignment with God's directive on tithes and offerings, as recorded in Malachi 4, is an imperative.

6. Authority to decree. A fifth factor to consider is a person's standing before the Lord to make the decree.

7. Apostolic alignment. Collaborate with godly mentors and allow His dream to mature in you!

PART 2

INTO
THE STORM

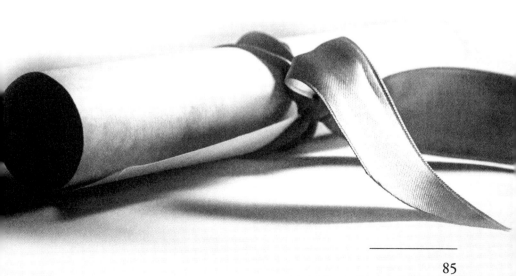

CHAPTER 4

INTO
THE STORM

"Fate whispers to the warrior, 'You cannot withstand the storm.' The warrior whispers back, 'I AM THE STORM.'" —Unknown

JOLENE AND I LED A TEAM THROUGH THE WHITE HOUSE just one day before the January 6 rampage that came to be known as the "Capitol Storm." The opportunity to tour America's highest seat of power had been granted to US at other key times in previous years. In fact, our private intercession through the West Wing once launched an international prayer project culminating with the Senate's confirmation of a Supreme Court justice.

But that day in January 2021, access had been relegated to a public walk-through. Cindy Jacobs, Chris Mitchell, Jr., and other amazing leaders joined us for this endeavor. Afterward we met with a senior official who had requested prayer.

Time stood still as we moved through stately rooms, accentuated by period paintings and diamond-like chandeliers, where some of the most decisive moments of history had occurred. It suddenly struck me this could be our last time here. At least for a while.

Maybe for this reason, virtually every step was marked by way too many photos. Obligatory masks made for unimpressive selfies. But thankfully they also concealed the fervency with which our lips were engaged in whispered prayer.

If ever there was a need for a governmental prayer decree, it was then. One that God would enforce to bring a turnaround. But as much as I longed for it, I sensed no guarantee. Which was honestly a mystery to us. For five years straight the turnarounds seemed unstoppable, in a way only the hand of the Lord could have produced. Then in 2020 challenges of similar magnitude simply refused to budge. *It seemed as though the hand of the Lord had suddenly lifted.*

The sense that God was not poised to intervene regarding the 2020 election results was carried through by Cindy Jacobs. I mentioned earlier that an administration official had requested prayer. When she asked what was ahead beyond January 5, Cindy was unusually forthright. The transition was occurring. It was time to seek another position. Her word proved correct.

There was, however, one decree I knew the Lord would both honor and fulfill whatever the circumstance. In my pocket was a simple covenant made up of exactly 777 words called the Mayflower Covenant Renewal. The text is based on the Mayflower Compact, originally ratified by the Pilgrims. My forefather Richard Warren was among the signers. On the 400th anniversary of the signing of this Compact, leaders gathered to see this covenant renewed for our time.

Our primary assignment at the White House was to present this covenant renewal before the Lord, asking Him to align the highest seats of power for His glory alone.

And, of course, grant a turnaround. Because genuine covenant with the Lord Jesus Christ makes His turnarounds inevitable, at least eventually.

> *"The covenant I have made with you, you shall not forget; nor shall you fear other gods. But the Lord your God you shall fear, and He shall deliver you from the hand of every adversary"* (2 Kings 17:38-39).

Covenant and Visitation

The Mayflower Covenant Renewal was written in Plymouth, Massachusetts, one week after the election, culminating in the early hours of November 11. This sacred date marked the 400th anniversary of the signing of the Mayflower Compact by the Pilgrims, committing the land and government "to the glory of God and the advancement of the Christian faith."

The Pilgrims had suffered great persecution at the hands of the monarchs of England. They came to these shores seeking religious freedom from what they felt was an antichrist expression of governance. It's important to note that the Pilgrims who arrived on America's shores were sent by an apostolic community preparing over decades for their greatest assignment from the Lord—to forge this new world in covenant with Jesus Christ as a beachhead against idolatry, or even antichrist dictatorship.

Messianic Jewish leader Asher Intrater notes that Jews in Europe referred to the Pilgrim community as "People of the covenant." According to Intrater, "the Pilgrims saw themselves as a new Israel, a nation in covenant with God."

Not a coincidence that the Mayflower Compact laid the foundation for democratic governance in the Western world.

To commemorate the anniversary, a group of key leaders, including Kevin Jessip, Michele Bachmann, Jody Wood, Chris Mitchell, Jr., Jeff and Kathy Pelton, Jim and Abby Abildness, Willie Jock, and others, had assembled together to pray for its renewal. We spent November 10 together, praying and strategizing in the first house erected by the Pilgrims.

Like myself, Kevin was also the descendant of a Pilgrim, actually John Robinson, who mentored the Pilgrims and then sent them to found the nation in covenant with God. We soon realized the Lord was inviting us to bring before Him a covenant of similar scope to the original May-flower Compact, encompassing its essence yet updated for this hour of history. Discussion propelled us into the evening.

Then to my surprise, just before midnight Michele Bachmann simply asked me to write it.

I stared for almost an hour at a blank scroll, glowing through the night on my screen. Thankfully, a midnight cry to the Lord eventually brought clarity, and I spent the first hours of November 11 writing this Mayflower Covenant Renewal. Much of the language of the original compact was included, as well as sentiments from the Gettysburg Address.

Later on the morning of November 11, we boarded the *Mayflower II*, a stunning replica of the original ship. The Spirit of God met us profoundly when we gathered in the hull to sign a copy of the original covenant. I was reminded how the Pilgrims included a description in the compact that they signed it "in the Presence of God and one another."

In the afternoon we returned to the Pilgrim House. As multitudes watched via live stream, we read, prayed through, and signed the new Mayflower Covenant Renewal, based on the original compact. Native American apostle Willie Jock helped tremendously with this sacred work. Until the moment he passed in 2021, Willie dedicated his life to gaining healing for his people from the generations of systemic abuse resulting from government policy. In my opinion his signature on the covenant of dedication carried the weight of the Lord Himself. It literally sealed the renewal.

It was amazing how the Lord moved in response. My friend Chris Mitchell, an apostolic leader from Virginia, had a profound experience with God as the covenant renewal was read. The glory of God literally enfolded him. For the sake of context, it's important to note that Chris is African American. Here's a description, in his own words.

On November 11ᵗʰ, 2020, I was privileged to be with Jon and Jolene in Plymouth, MA, to commemorate the 400ᵗʰ anniversary of the signing of the Mayflower Compact. I remember being keenly aware of the significance of the time and feeling the reverential fear of the Lord. As we gathered onboard the *Mayflower II* during the morning hours on the 11ᵗʰ to sign the original Mayflower Compact that sense of awe remained. It was a very powerful moment.

However, what occurred later that afternoon was one of the most profound experiences I have ever had with the Lord.

I was seated in the historic home that was hosting our meetings. Jon was downstairs preparing to declare a revised version of the original compact, given to him by the Holy Spirit the night before. As he read the words publicly for the first time, the tangible, weighty presence God's glory filled the upstairs room where I was seated.

Immediately I went into an encounter where I saw the Mayflower Compact out in front of me. As I watched, it unraveled and stretched out, wrapping itself around me like a blanket. I was actually embraced by this foundational covenant of our Nation! It embraced me, bringing me into to its substance and inheritance.

I immediately knew that this experience was not just simply for me personally. I believe it was a declaration that in this renewed expression of our nation's covenant with God, He is bringing those who once stood on the outside of His dream called America into their rightful place. Those who have felt disconnected and disenfranchised from the promise of this nation. Those who have stood on the outside for whatever reasons, are now being brought into the inheritance ordained for them in this land.

Our nation cannot fully wear the mantle of freedom and justice it is called to until it fulfills its creed, "That all men are created equal and endowed by their Creator with certain unalienable

> In this renewed expression of our nation's covenant with God, He is bringing those who once stood on the outside of His dream called America into their rightful place.

rights..." I believe the historic breaches that have frustrated this expression of our covenantal foundations are being healed. And God is releasing every kindred, tribe, and tongue into their ordained place.

The experience Chris had with the Lord moves my heart more deeply than even some of my own. It is the summation of all we have worked to see. The inheritance of this nation does not belong to self-appointed elites, but to every tongue, tribe, and nation in the Lord. If you have ever felt distant from this legacy, or disenfranchised from the promise of America, the Lord's eyes are on you. He wants to extend the covering of His covenant over you![1]

A similar occurrence to what Chris experienced came as the Lord moved in a small multiracial congregation in Southeast Georgia called Remnant Church, pastored by Jamie and Redonnia Jackson. After the Mayflower Covenant Renewal was first read there, a Native American man moved forward and politely interrupted the service.

"Excuse me, but I would like to sign my name on this covenant," he said, with tears in his eyes. "Is that okay?"

We immediately scrambled for a pen.

The Native American brother was soon joined by a black woman legendary for her fiery intercession. "For the first time I finally feel like I'm part," she simply said. That moved everybody else to tears. Then spontaneously, just about every person of color in the building lined up, with the rest of us fitting in somewhere in the mix. The signing was completely unplanned.

Every tongue, tribe, and nation joined together in Him. That's the power of God's covenant! That's the dream of His heart for America.

2019 Vision—Reconstitution of Scrolls

Long before writing the Mayflower Covenant Renewal, the Lord had actually shown me a vision of a renewed version coming from His throne. I saw stacks of crumpled up pieces of paper on a huge table, which I knew symbolically to be the Table of the Lord. Jesus was sitting behind the table, placing each document with great care into the "sea of glass" pictured before His throne. I was literally watching a baptism—of crumpled up scrolls!

In the glassy sea these decrees unfolded, expanded, and became clear again. They were reconstituted. Then they were rereleased, often to the people and nations who had initially rejected them.

And in the vision, the first scroll I saw reconstituted was actually the Mayflower Compact. It was wild to later be asked to write a revised version of the compact for release in our hour. On the very 400th anniversary! Can't make this stuff up.

Here's a principle worth remembering: God's genuine "turnaround decrees" do not have their origins on earth but rather Heaven. And in this season He is granting access to peer into these scrolls, and even see many of them released to define our future.

Hindsight Is 20/20

Almost to the date of our prayer tour through the White House, two months had passed since the 2020 elections. Grief initially overcame many in the Body of Christ. This was followed by perhaps the most intense season of concerted prayer since 9-11-01. Which was great. Except for the fact that the election had already occurred.

It seemed that before the elections many believers simply assumed Donald Trump would regain the presidency without much of a fight. The words of many prophets seemed to fuel that assumption. Instead the political chess game over the 2020 elections had been played with a ruthlessness perhaps never seen in the history of our land. What many term "the Deep State" proved to be a more formidable foe to constitutional governance than most Americans could have imagined.

As the old adage goes, "hindsight is 20/20." In this case, literally.

Let me begin by stating clearly that President Trump was, in many cases, his own worst enemy. Internal and external divisiveness, narcissism, vilification of rivals, and diplomacy by Twitter all took a huge toll on the American people.

As we shared in *White House Watchmen*, the Lord had spoken to us that the primary election issue before the throne was whether or not President Trump would embrace his invited role to stand as a father to all Americans. An Eliakim. The goal required for him to attain is all the more relevant for us to attain. Like Jacob of old, we are all called to shift from dysfunction and deception that marked our past into a new identity as Israel, prince with God and father of the covenant nation.

That said, none of this justifies the onslaught that began from the moment Donald Trump was elected. High level leaders within government, the media, and even the intelligence communities collaborated together to produce extreme propaganda to discredit his presidency, again from the very moment he was elected.

You must understand. *This was a collaborative effort to take down a sitting president of the United States.* Not just by a fringe group bent on sedition. Instead, this effort was mobilized both from America's most influential media institutions and from within the highest halls of our government itself.

Most of the propaganda generated, especially allegations of Russia collusion, proved completely false. Yet it was used as the primary excuse to sabotage his administration from the very outset.

Amazingly, none of the Pulitzer Prizes won for validating the false allegations were returned. In fact, few have genuinely been held accountable for deceiving and dividing the nation for personal or partisan gain.

Manufactured disinformation is nothing new, especially in the intelligence world. But our nation, including journalism and even our own intelligence communities, was founded on the bedrock of another motto. An ancient declaration by Jesus is actually prominently engraved in the lobby of CIA headquarters: *"And ye shall know the truth, and the truth shall make you free"* (John 8:32).

Regardless of the political winds, the measure of truth we as a society embrace determines the future of our freedom. So there's really a problem when the highest-ranking members of the intelligence community leak purposefully deceptive information about our nation's president. It is only magnified when a biased media reports these leaks as truth without ever verifying them. Keep in mind that these false allegations became "justification" for two separate impeachment trials.

What is truly scary is how many leaders seemed to assume an elitist right of rulership of America, and then blew out anyone who got in the way of their agenda.

That kind of propaganda is how the Nazis gained power. And when government institutions become extensions of political control, the inevitable result is authoritarianism instead of freedom. Just ask residents of North Korea, Venezuela, or Cuba. In fact, some of the most vehement warnings are coming from Cuban Americans who are recognizing the same nation-destabilizing tactics once employed in the communist takeover of their nation. That should really give you pause.

In addition we were also dealing with a multitude of variants from a manufactured virus originating from China, now our chief rival on the global stage. It was probably not a coincidence that COVID-19 emerged during an election year. In any case, the ensuing crisis has been ruthlessly maximized by politicians to restrict, or in some cases even negate, our constitutional freedoms. Especially the freedom of religion.

Not surprisingly, after the elections, strong claims of fraud, accompanied by equally strong prophetic words, conveyed that the election wasn't yet over. Jolene and I remained unconvinced of their full veracity. But at least a dimension of the election was in our opinion absolutely fraudulent.

Let's evaluate the situation. Given the extreme deception, overreach, and subterfuge employed nonstop through Trump's presidency, why would any rational human being fully believe the election results were not somehow manipulated?

It's like the famous scene from one of the Star Wars movies. *You don't need to see the voter's identification. This is not the evidence you're looking for. There's nothing to see here. Go about your business. Move along...*

Through the efforts of the administration, in so many ways America genuinely began to turn for the good. Further, the 45th president purposely disrupted plans and policies of the global elite like few in history.

So again, given the nonstop disinformation campaigns generated against the administration since the moment Trump was elected, we remain wary that the 2020 elections were free from manipulation.

Disinformation Sourced from the Body of Christ

But in integrity, we must also look at disinformation sourced from the Body of Christ. For instance, many prophets prophesied a Trump victory in lucid detail—before, during, and after the election, and even over the entire year following. Though we were inspired by many of their sentiments, many predictions proved false. Many were sensationalized. Further, many storylines, such as the QAnon phenomenon, combined some accurate intelligence with conspiratorial misinformation that propelled leaders off course. Even some prophets.

Prophetic disinformation is damaging. It can lead multitudes into deception. It also sabotages our spiritual warfare, as we are called to wage war according to the prophecies entrusted to us (see 1 Tim. 1:18). But with wrong revelation or prayer targets, our efforts become largely ineffective. We pray wrongly, we decree wrongly, and we set our hopes according to misdirected expectations.

Maybe it would give some pause if leaders knew the depth of heartbreak experienced by many Trump administration officials, including strong believers in our home group, who leaned into many of these words for direction. I'm by no means seeking to put limitations on either the message or the messenger. As a community we simply need to keep humble, keep accountable, and keep teachable.

> Prophetic disinformation is damaging. It can lead multitudes into deception. It also sabotages our spiritual warfare, as we are called to wage war according to the prophecies entrusted to us.

Because only the truth will make us free. In Jesus it is our most valuable commodity.

My overall conclusion is that we were wrestling against a magnitude of evil that most leaders simply did not perceive until it was too late. I believe many of the words were essentially correct in substance, but wrong in the timing of their fulfillment. The Lord will redeem, of course, because He sees our hearts. And the intercession mobilized has truly gone a long way toward bringing God's redemptive exposure of corruption.

But we've all got to come up higher. Jolene and me first! There's simply too much at stake.

Prophetically, the Lord warned Jolene and me about the 2020 elections far in advance of the crisis. Our book *White House Watchmen* was written with an immediate goal of mobilizing concerted forerunning prayer to counter the battle we sensed before the elections.

Because, as we warned, the election itself was a turning point of a magnitude very few were perceiving.

Watchman, What of the Night?

Here's the backstory. On Thanksgiving evening 2019, the Lord encountered me in our condominium overlooking Washington, DC. I was excited for the prospects ahead in 2020. But as I began to pray, an overwhelming heaviness encompassed my spirit. Internally, the alarm began to sound. And Holy Spirit simply said to me, *Watchman, what of the night?* I suddenly knew we were entering into a midnight hour as a nation.

It's important to watch how God alerts you to times and seasons ahead. Be sure to record it as a reference for your future!

It was at the same window back in 2017 that Holy Spirit had spoken to me about the coming midnight hour for America, with a series of "midnight crises" beginning as of 2020. As we shared before, a midnight cry in a midnight watch would lead to a midnight turnaround. How we confronted these challenges, and overcame them, would become a prototype of victory for believers in the very end of days.

And on Thanksgiving evening 2019, the Spirit of God alerted me that these challenges would soon begin.

The prospect stunned me. At the time the "midnight cry" word was far from my remembrance. Instead my focus was locked on the 2020 elections, and especially the week beyond, which again marked the 400th anniversary of America's covenant with God.

That said, the warning was very clear. Every page of *White House Watchmen*, beginning with the introduction below, was birthed out of this warning.

Prophetically I've known for many years that what we decide in 2020 impacts our nation in a way that few other times in history ever have—for generations. Like the Pilgrims' original voyage, it is a threshold from which there is no return. Will America choose open defiance of God? Will a vicious storm drive us off course, or even reverse the vulnerable progress we've made? Or will we honor the covenantal foundations entrusted to us, and complete the turnaround that secures our inheritance for decades?...

This prophetic warning, from the introduction of *White House Watchmen*, really provokes my heart given the challenges now unfolding before our eyes. Which direction has America embraced—open defiance of the Lord? A realignment with our covenantal foundations? Or perhaps, like the Pilgrims in their hour of crisis, our best intentions were sideswiped by a turbulent storm which blew us all off course?

These questions are vital to answer if you and I are to gain the spiritual authority necessary to catalyze God's intended turnaround in this hour. Jolene and I are convinced of the third option. A vicious storm, summoned both from without and within, exploiting atmospheric conditions which had already made us intensely vulnerable, forced a change in the intended trajectory.

As with the Pilgrims, it nearly shipwrecked us.

January 6—Into the Storm

Through a whispered directive by Holy Spirit, Jolene and I had been warned not to attend the January 6 rally and march. Instead, like most Americans we watched the events unfold on television at home, gripped by a horrified awe.

Unlike most Americans, we could see the Capitol building in the distance as we watched.

Let me clarify prophetically that the march itself, from the White House to the Capitol, was right. The breaching of the US Capitol was a trap. A peaceful, lawful protest suddenly morphed into an overwhelming storm as multitudes burst through barriers and flooded the US Capitol grounds. Some even gained entry to the building. This occurred at the very moment a joint session of Congress had convened to review the election results. Vice President Pence was onsite to oversee the process, as lawmakers began hearings on whether or not to ratify Biden as president or delay the decision until further allegations of fraud could be properly reviewed.

The event became known as the Capitol Storm.

Maybe the storm was not physical, like the one which besieged the Pilgrims. But it produced a similar result. The movement to invoke constitutional protections against election fraud was blown way off course.

Instead of inspiring the lawmakers to allot more time to review viable allegations, the Capitol Storm protest convinced them to seal the deal. As soon as it was deemed safe for the lawmakers to return, Joe Biden was confirmed as the 46th president of the United States.

Then our nation's lawmakers decided to erect a massive security barrier. In a manner usually reserved for battlefield headquarters, perimeter fencing completely encircled Capitol Hill, with razor wire crowning every inch. Both Constitution and Independence Avenues were blocked. The National Guard openly brandished M-16s while keeping vigilant watch. Passersby and even government workers were met with aggressive directives.

But again, this was not the Green Zone of Baghdad or Kabul. Instead it was the very symbol of American democracy. Freedom itself seemed to be under siege, long after any legitimate threat had passed.

Conquering the Raging Storm

That said, we can learn a lot from how the Pilgrims faced their storm, a powerful nor'easter which blindsided them off of the coast of Cape Cod. At first they resolved to navigate their way through, fighting every burst of wind and wave. But it soon became clear that doing so would only decimate their overcrowded boat. To preserve both lives and mission, the Pilgrims found refuge in a natural harbor near the tip of Cape Cod. And after intense debate, they decided simply to pick up their overarching mission right where they left off.

Following the instructions of their mentor and apostle John Robinson, they bowed on their faces before the Lord and thanked Him for safe passage. They came into agreement to unite, settle, pray, and build in their newfound home. The Pilgrims then entered into covenant with God and each other, committing their new land and government "to the glory of God and the advancement of the Christian faith" through the Mayflower Compact.

And in a way unimaginable to the weary founders who wrote it, this decree, and the fragile democracy it birthed, eventually turned the entirety of Western civilization toward freedom.

In our nation today, a raging storm has blown us off course. The structural integrity of the vessel, which brought us so close to the destiny we know the Lord intends for us, has become severely compromised.

But the mission remains exactly the same. Let's dream. Let's pray. Let's rebuild, right where we are. And let's complete the turnaround assigned to our watch.

> The structural integrity of the vessel, which brought us so close to the destiny we know the Lord intends for us, has become severely compromised. But the mission remains exactly the same. Let's dream. Let's pray. Let's rebuild, right where we are.

I pray the words of the Revised Mayflower Compact, a summation of America's covenant with God, will inspire you toward this end. It is a decree for this hour. You will recognize language from the original Mayflower Compact as well as the Gettysburg Address.

And know this: Just as with the Pilgrims, against all odds His covenant will prevail in our time. Because God remembers. And ultimately it is He, not the storm, who establishes our course.

No King but Jesus...

Turnaround Decree 4: Mayflower Covenant Renewal

Written and signed November 11, 2020
in Plymouth Massachusetts

In the name of God, Amen. We whose names are underwritten, loyal subjects of our Sovereign Jesus Christ, by the grace of the God of Israel, Great Britain, etc. Having undertaken for the Glory of God and the advancement of the Christian Faith and Honor of our King and Kingdom, a sacred endeavor to reset the United States of America's covenant with our Creator, establishing this covenant on the 400th anniversary of the Mayflower Compact; do by these presents solemnly and mutually, in the Presence of God and one of another, hereby request and receive the very hand of God in the reconstitution of this covenant of marriage between Jesus Christ and our land.

We acknowledge with solemn gratitude that You have granted our request for an annulment of all covenants with other gods, with death and hell, empowered by unjust bloodshed, which we and our forefathers had made and succumbed to, resulting in our present condition. We seek you now to establish us in Your covenant of Life. And with all solemnity and deference to Your Majesty, we request that Your Glory, the Presence and Power of Holy Spirit, might now return and reside again in this land, releasing awakening, union, moral clarity and LIFE.

In a larger sense, we realize that our pleas alone can not dedicate—can not consecrate—can not hallow—this ground. The brave men and women, living and dead, who struggled here, have consecrated it, far above our poor power to add or detract. And as one small candle can light a thousand, so the light here kindled has been passed unto all successive generations—first because You keep covenant with us, and show great mercy.

With this at heart, for consideration in this Petition, we present to You the Covenantal legacy of the Pilgrims, who on 11-11, 1620 committed the land and government to "the glory of God and the advancement of the Christian faith," according to the Mayflower Compact.

And we present to You the Covenantal legacy of the Huguenots who came to this land with the same intention—whose blood was spilled and mission aborted—whose founder died chanting Psalm 132, begging Your Majesty that this land would be a "dwelling place for the Mighty God of Jacob."

And we present to You the covenant of the Virginia Company, whose chaplain declared the dedication of this land for the acceleration of Christ's Gospel to the world, even sealing it with a planted cross;

And we present to You the covenant of William Penn, whose devotion to the principles of Christ in governance revolutionized the nation and world;

And we present to You the original intent of many Host people of the Land—who agreed from the beginning that both ownership and stewardship belongs to their Creator and Father. Who sought with reverence to honor the Laws of Nature, and Nature's God. To whom You endowed great wisdom, even to convey and implement principles of democratic governance that framed the United States Constitution.

And finally, we present to You the legacy of the Seed of Abraham, by which Your Covenant with Israel and Mankind has been perpetuated. Our gratitude is immeasurable that You have chosen to graft us into this Covenant! To this end, we fully commit our covenantal stewardship to resource the dream of Your heart for Israel, the Jewish people, and for the nations.

Having undertaken the sacred task of repairing our Nation's founding covenants with our Creator; and having diligently and wholeheartedly sought forgiveness for breaches of said covenants, offensive to God and detrimental to mankind; we now combine these founding covenants as one Sacred Consecration of this land, the United States of America and all of its territories, to the Lord Jesus Christ.

It is for us the living, now, to be dedicated here to the unfinished work which all who struggled before us have thus far so nobly advanced—that this nation, under God, shall have a new birth of freedom—and that government of the people, by the people, for the people, shall not perish from the earth.

And as You have engraved us in the palm of Your hand; as You have granted us this gracious judgment in favor of the saints, this Verdict of Your redemption; so we again request and receive the Hand of God in marriage, unto whom we promise all affection, loyalty and sacred obedience.

In witness whereof we have hereunto subscribed our names in Plymouth, Massachusetts, on the 11th day of November, 2020, and afterward across the land. No King but Jesus!

Signed _____ Date _____

SEVEN ON A SCROLL:
White House Watchmen—Words that Came to Pass

1. "For 2020, Brown Wins!" Prophecy in fall 2019 submitted privately then publicly, conveying that various shades of brown were going to carry the 2020 elections, came to pass.

2. America's Midnight Hour—given in 2017. By 2020, a series of midnight crises would occur, similar to biblical descriptions of the end times. With the onset of COVID, challenges within government, etc., this seems to be on point.

3. Blue Wave Coming. Wave of Defilement Checked: "I will not allow your defiled waters to direct the course of the nation any more."

4. Cuomo Down—Jolene saw that as with pharaoh, former NY governor Andrew Cuomo defied the Lord in word and deed, and even legalized infanticide in New York State. As prophesied, God brought pharaoh down.

5. Breakthroughs Overcoming Abortion

6. "New Era of Victory"—we wrote that despite setbacks, the victory God intends for our land will prevail. It's already coming to pass.

7. "In the year King Uzziah died I saw the Lord..." The last chapter, on the governmental glory, focused on Isaiah 6 and the thrones shaking due to the removal of the king. It was then that the Lord unveiled to Isaiah His unshakeable throne, and cleansed Isaiah's defiled lips.

CHAPTER 5

CALL 911

"Jules, this is Brian. Listen, I'm on an airplane that's been hijacked. If things don't go well, and it's not looking good, I just want you to know that I absolutely love you." —Airline passenger and former Navy pilot Brian Sweeney, September 11, 2001

NEW ERAS ARE OFTEN MARKED BY DEFINING EVENTS, both evil and good, which remain largely unperceived until they appear in the earth. The birth of Christ. The Protestant Reformation. The American Revolution. The rise of Hitler. The rebirth of Israel. The Jesus revolution. The unleashing of the digital age. Or 911.

Most people barely grasp the significance of events while they are unfolding before their very eyes. But as custodians of Heaven's closest secrets, God's prophets are often shown epoch-defining events before they occur. Their words ahead of time provide context our busied hearts desperately need afterward. And within their prophetic perspectives you will always find key decrees to gain His intended turnaround.

Here's one story.

On September 11, 2001, Islamist terrorists thrust America and the world into a new era of history. Hijacked airplanes were turned into deadly missiles and thrust into the greatest symbols of America's economic and military might. The Twin Towers of the World Trade Center exploded, then completely collapsed. The western wall of the Pentagon disintegrated. A total of 2,996 people died. And America responded by charging into a 20-year war.

> ...as custodians of Heaven's closest secrets, God's prophets are often shown epoch-defining events before they occur.

Approximately two weeks before 9-11, our friend Ceci Sheets, wife of Dutch Sheets, dreamed that she was pregnant. Before she could even grasp the news, she looked down and realized her pregnancy had suddenly come to full term. Ceci entered into travail, with nobody around to assist.

"Call 911! Call 911!" Ceci exclaimed in the dream. "My baby is about to be born! And there is nobody to help deliver my child. The experts are needed at this time!"

The prescience of this dream, just days before September 11, is haunting. But when you realize Ceci's husband Dutch was passing through New York City that very morning on a governmental prayer tour, the dream becomes a marker of history.

Dutch was leading a prayer journey called the Kettle Tour, focused on historic roots of awakening, covenant, and government throughout the northeast. Dutch was strongly focused on two prophetic messages: the Isaiah 22:22 movement of Eliakim and governmental authority and a movement of Acts 3:19 repentance and turnaround to release God's intended destiny for our land. As Dutch thundered relentlessly through the journey, Acts 3:19 can be translated: "Repent and return, so that your sins may be washed away, so that times of refreshing—literally, the blowing again of the breath of God, the breath of birthing or new beginnings—may come from the presence of the Lord."

Not coincidentally, both messages are key for 2022 and beyond. Keys of governmental authority are being entrusted to God's Eliakims, those devoted to fathering and mentoring instead of gaining at the expense of those they are called to serve.

And the breath of God is blowing again.

A high-level group of leaders and intercessors was selected for the Kettle Tour, including Lou Engle, Will Ford, and others. I was honored to join the journey as well.

The tour was named after an old iron kettle Will had inherited from his father, who in turn had inherited from his slave forefathers. They would cook in the kettle during the day. But in the middle of the night they would pray into the kettle, ensuring their most desperate cries for freedom were muffled from the ears of slavemasters nearby.

It was passed down that Will's slave forefathers had a standing rule. They never prayed for freedom from slavery for themselves. Instead they prayed only for their sons and daughters and successive generations.

The iron kettle became a profound, poignant symbol of the bowls of prayer pictured in Revelation 5. Dutch, Will, and the team felt summoned to this East Coast journey because of a sense the bowls were going to tip.

Little did I know that this journey would mark my own emergence into national prophetic ministry. The journey became an unexpected birthing for me. The Lord gave me an impacting prophecy that turned out to be similar to Ceci's dream in its prescience. I saw a coming "martyrs harvest" for New England and the nation. The Elijah List published the word on September 5, just six days before 9-11. More on this in a moment.

We were leaving from New Jersey to New England when Ceci called to share the "Call 911" dream. In fact, our team was exploring the meaning as our bus crossed the Hudson River on the Tappan Zee Bridge. I will never forget the moment when the New York skyscrapers came into view, with the Twin Towers forming a massive "11" above the others. None of us had any idea we were seeing the towers for the last time.

Call 911—The Meaning

Two decades later, the message from Ceci's dream has vital keys for today. Let's start with a few obvious perceptions.

First and foremost, the dream conveyed a real-time prophetic warning about the coming 9-11 attacks. We are moving into a season where real-time prophetic revelation must not only be accurately received, but accurately interpreted. Our very lives may depend on it.

A secondary purpose of the dream was to convey warnings about threats faced by our children. Both their innocence and their process of maturity must be guarded. I hope you can see how greatly God desires to preserve their destinies!

Travailing prayer brings to birth God's covenant purposes. On a larger scale, the dream warned of peril in this process. We remain in a season of intense travail for what Abraham Lincoln termed "a new birth of freedom" for our land. Yet as in the days of Pharaoh and Herod, our most powerful enemies now stand at the very gateways of America's birth canal, seeking to abort the freedom movement God is bringing forth. Experts are needed to protect the child!

Maybe that's why, from the moment Ceci conveyed the dream, Dutch focused on Psalm 91 as a primary promise being released to God's people. Dwelling in the secret place of the Most High, gaining deliverance from the snare of the trapper and the deadly pestilence. A companion verse is Amos 9:11, which conveys the potential for God's protection on a national level through the restoration of the Tabernacle of David. We'll dive into both passages as the chapter culminates.

But on the most basic level, 9-11 is a call for help in an emergency. The "Call 911" dream conveys the urgent need to immediately pray, to cry out for intervention until it comes. Hopefully before it's too late.

Power Shift in the Oval Office

Joe Biden crossed the Potomac River in a slow-moving presidential motorcade after paying tribute to veterans at the Arlington National Cemetery. It was Inauguration Day 2021. Jolene and I watched the procession from our home overlooking the city. His next stop was the White House.

Earlier in the day we were among a few hundred supporters and administration officials attending a departure ceremony for President Trump at Andrews Air Force Base. Boisterous rally songs blared from the sound system as the *Marine One* helicopter hovered, landed, and taxied close to the podium before escorting the entourage on to the tarmac. Donald Trump, accompanied by his wife Melania, gave his final speech as president. Then in typical Trumpian fashion, he finished his message with a wave, mouthed the words *thank you*, and said on the microphone, "Have a nice life."

Air Force One departed.

Swearing-in ceremonies at the barricaded Capitol commenced shortly after. The highest seats of power in US government were successfully transferred.

Soon after the motorcade arrived, Joe Biden took his seat behind the Resolute Desk for the very first time as president of the United States. The date, January 20, 2021, marked only two weeks since our final prayer tour through the White House, marked by a desperate plea for God to remember His covenant with our nation.

President Biden's first official act exemplified the power of making decrees from his seat of authority. Four years of ceaseless efforts by Trump policy makers became crumpled up pieces of paper discarded from his desk. It was a heartbreaking turnaround. Overthrowing the historic Trump-era restrictions on government-funded abortion was at the very top of the stack. Followed by the immediate cessation of the border wall project, and the reempowerment of unrestricted immigration. The deluge of migrants that followed soon became a humanitarian crisis.

This was followed by the cancellation of the Keystone XL pipeline. The decision has not only caused oil prices to spike dramatically, but it set in motion a rapid acceleration of inflation across the spectrum of consumer goods that continues to this day.

And there was so much more. It was astonishing how quickly so many of the godly precedents set by the previous administration were reversed. And the very fact that Biden utilized executive orders to accomplish his goal violated his most vehement pledge during his campaign.

But now he was in office. Probably his handlers realized that from the moment he took over, they needed to counter emerging stereotypes by making him look assertive and in control.

Biden's actions were the exact antithesis of the turnarounds we witnessed with our own eyes during the Trump administration. Here's a backstory.

Daniel 7:22—Unleashing Governmental Turnarounds

On July 22, 2014, what we've come to call the Turnaround Verdict was released by the Lord from Faneuil Hall in historic Boston. Again, from Daniel 7:22, judgment is rendered in favor of the saints, restraining the enemy and releasing the saints to possess the Kingdom. The results from decreeing this verdict have been both consistent and comprehensive in scope, far beyond our wildest expectations. Including a last-minute election turnaround which, to all our surprise, catapulted businessman Donald Trump into America's highest office.

What we did not realize is how this same verdict would also propel Jolene, myself, and other Christian leaders into America's halls of power—providing breakthrough prayer, insight, and counsel in the midst of immense conflict. We in turn had a front-row seat to many extraordinary turnarounds initiated by the administration in virtually every sphere of government, correlated to years of unwavering prayer.

Economic turnaround brought the lowest unemployment records in American history for women and minorities. Until COVID hit, the economy continued to grow at record pace, upending all predictions.

Unprecedented judicial reform was also secured, with three Supreme Court justices seated as well as 220 federal judges.

The military was restrengthened after years of decline. Trump even created a new branch, the US Space Force.

In diplomacy, the Abraham Accords established historic break-throughs toward Mideast peace through open alliances once considered impossible. The sovereignty of Israel was also honored as the US embassy was moved to Jerusalem, and the Golan Heights was officially recognized as part of the land.

Trump and Pence also formed the most pro-life administration in American history. That's a true turnaround for sure. Policy regarding abortion was tackled with both compassion and principle. Government funding was cut nationally and globally as a means of disempowering the industry's vast overreach.

Then there was the handling of the COVID-19 crisis. Let's keep in mind that this virus was most likely developed as a weapon of war. Probably it was accidentally leaked. But still it was engineered to maximize harm to human beings, including you and your loved ones.

Vaccines were created in record time under the supervision of the administration and have proven effective overall in stemming the most damaging symptoms of the virus. In balance, it should also be noted that many have suffered from initial reactions to the vaccine. And the long-term effects have yet to be known.

Please note that neither Jolene nor I believe government should be allowed to force any US citizen to get a vaccine. There is simply no constitutional provision for this.

Now more than ever we must understand that all gains in science, the tech world, and government can be stewarded to accelerate good or evil across the globe. That's why we need competent governmental leaders who genuinely know the Lord, seek His direction, and embrace Judeo-Christian values from the core of their beings.

So much is at stake. The Lord has summoned us all to come up higher.

Let me mention a few other turnarounds from the Trump administration. Unexpectedly, religious freedom became a pillar of diplomacy on a global level. Policies set in motion by President Trump with Secretary of State Mike Pompeo and Religious Freedom Ambassador Sam Brownback rescued this constitutional decree from the totalitarian trash bin. The horrific persecution against people of faith, especially at the hands of radical jihadists, became exposed nationally and internationally through religious freedom summits, including a precedent-setting gathering hosted by President Trump himself at the United Nations General Assembly.

Speaking of which, Al Qaeda and ISIS, perhaps the two strongest terror networks in the world, both of whom brutally persecuted Christians and other religious minorities, were decisively defeated by US forces as demanded by President Trump.

Finally, in yet another astonishing turnaround, the Trump administration negotiated a power-sharing agreement between the Afghan government and rebel Taliban leaders set to bring closure to America's 20-year war. A timetable had been established with specific conditions to be achieved and maintained by both parties before the US military would initiate the withdrawal.

Turning Down the Turnaround

A few months before the 20th anniversary of the September 11 terrorist strikes, President Biden strongly asserted his executive authority regarding Afghanistan. Most thought he would build on the framework handed to him by the Trump administration. Instead, he turned down the turnaround, demanding the US military withdraw our troops way ahead of the timetable previously agreed upon by all parties. This created one of the most heartbreaking policy failures in modern American history.

President Biden overruled his closest advisors in military and intelligence to force his decision through, just as Taliban aggression began to accelerate dramatically. The timing could not have been worse. Knowing Biden was prioritizing a quick exit before the 9-11 anniversary, the terror group no only pushed the barriers of the power-sharing agreement but plowed right through them.

And their calculus proved correct. Without US forces to back up the Afghan military, the Taliban surged in battle. Afghan soldiers across the nation simply surrendered—and then ran for their lives. In one day the entirety of Afghanistan, including the capital of Kabul, was ceded back to the very terrorists who empowered Al Qaeda to strike on 9-11.

Suddenly more than 120,000 Americans became trapped in the land they were serving.

"We completed one of the biggest airlifts in history," President Biden asserted in a press conference on August 31, the deadline set for America's withdrawal. "The bottom line: ninety percent of Americans in Afghanistan who wanted to leave were able to leave!"

According to Biden's own statistics, this meant that one out of every ten Americans in Afghanistan was actually left behind. The outrage of the American people across the aisles was immediate and sustained.

Astonishingly, American citizens continue to be channeled out secretly by private special ops teams, while hundreds still await rescue.

Meanwhile, Afghanistan continues spiraling into chaos. The national economy is collapsing. Brutal abuse of women and children has sky-rocketed again, even though officially prohibited. The rights of women continue to be revoked. Public hangings have been reinstated. And Christians in the land are again being meticulously tracked, hunted, and martyred.

Perhaps most dire, the nation is again becoming a haven for barbaric terrorists similar to those who initiated 9-11.

State of the Union

Looking back, the terrorists who took down the Twin Towers and exploded into the Pentagon were targeting much more than the mortar and steel of our buildings. They targeted the essence of who we are as Americans. Freedom. Inclusiveness. Justice. Civil discourse. Generosity. Innovation. Prosperity. The dignity and worth of every human being. Proactive governance by consent of the governed rather than total-itarianism. Balance of power. Freedom of the press. Religious liberty. Protection of the family unit. An inherent goodness based on a strong moral compass. A godly patriotism which unites rather than divides. Hope for the future. Resolve to overcome.

No King but Jesus.

The 9-11 tragedy initially united all Americans with a fierce resolve to protect, defend, and perpetuate these values. It is important to note that they are sourced from our covenantal foundation as a nation under God.

And we've made a lot of progress. As an Israeli general pointed out to me recently, a lot of mistakes were made. But America still took took down both Al Qaeda and ISIS, two of the strongest and most brutal terror networks in modern history. These victories are worthy of our highest honor. And so are the men and women, known and unknown to us, who sacrificed so much to secure them.

On the negative side, our initial resolve to protect the homeland soon became a justification to compromise our freedoms. Over two decades we have seen our privacies eroded and our constitutional right to believe, speak, and live according to biblical values severely marginalized.

Remember that our founders lived and died to gain these rights for us. They are what made us great. And the highest goal of the 9-11 terrorists was the erosion of these very values.

On our watch we have largely capitulated to a surveillance state—with a "woke" culture now seeking to dictate principles that are often completely contrary to biblical truths, biblical values, and really the heart of God.

The biggest casualty seems to be truth itself. As mentioned, manufactured disinformation has become normalized. Big tech has been given virtually free rein to program our culture the way former generations learned to program their computers. And astonishingly, today the greatest resistance to protecting America's cherished values is now coming from our elected officials.

How has this worked for us? Consider the current state of our union. A godly love of country is at an all-time

> ...the terrorists who took down the Twin Towers and exploded into the Pentagon were targeting much more than the mortar and steel of our buildings. They targeted the essence of who we are as Americans.

low, while distrust of government is at an all-time high. Economic woes are overtaking the nation. Socialism is gaining in popularity, and the totalitarian agenda behind it is now actually being embraced as a viable alternative to our constitutional republic. As mentioned, in many public school systems our children are being mandated to choose their sexuality as early as kindergarten.

Not coincidentally, biblical morality is spiraling. Most American churches are struggling to survive. And our nation is more deeply divided than any time in recent history.

Through the previous twenty years, American society became "woke." But we have not really awakened, nor have we genuinely turned to the Lord. We have largely chosen the wrong turnaround.

The Teshuvah Turnaround

One of the strongest words for "turnaround" in the Hebrew language is *teshuvah*. Not coincidentally, the word also means "repentance." Covenant restoration is the foundation for any genuine turnaround from the hand of the Lord. Repentance or *teshuvah* brings us into realignment with His covenant, so that we become positioned to receive the blessing He holds out.

The apostle Peter emphasized this in his landmark message after Holy Spirit fire fell at Pentecost. Not coincidentally it is again the primary message Dutch Sheets and our team carried through the Northeast just prior to September 11, 2001.

> *"Repent and return, so that your sins may be washed away, so that times of refreshing may come from the presence of the Lord"* (Acts 3:19).

I believe the awakening alarm is now sounding again, with an unmistakable call to repentance. Our great invitation is to forsake our delusion and the pride that fuels it. Let's return to covenant with the Lord Jesus Christ. Let's secure again His covering as a nation under God!

Prophetically, the Spirit of God is warning about the potential of another attack on our soil, of a similar or even greater magnitude than 9-11-01. It's a sense I have not been able to shake. The Lord has shown me no timetable at present. But the attempted sabotage by the enemy seems sooner rather than later. A derailment of our free-market economy is targeted. And it may sound trite, but the bombs bursting in air will in the end give proof that our flag is still there.

> Covenant restoration is the foundation for any genuine turnaround from the hand of the Lord. Repentance or *teshuvah* brings us into realignment with His covenant, so that we become positioned to receive the blessing He holds out.

Whether this attack can be mitigated or even prevented is not clear either. Please pray. Enter into repentance over your sins, and the sins of the nation. Call 911. We need the Lord to restore His covenant covering over the land!

9-11—Jon's Emergence into Prophetic Ministry

A ruthless enemy is seeking to force an abortion of God's covenant purposes in America. Meanwhile, the Lord desires to grant a new birth of freedom for our covenant nation. Now more than ever, the experts are needed at this time.

God's passionate intentions on this are pictured in a prophetic experience I received back in 1996. It remains the most impactful of my life. Maybe not coincidentally, as mentioned the prophetic marked my entrance into national prophetic ministry when it was published on the Elijah List just days prior to the September 11 tragedy.

Back in 1996 I was praying over Provincetown, the historic Cape Cod harbor where the Pilgrims wrote the Mayflower Compact, when I had the vision. A local pastor had asked me to seek the Lord with him over a recurring dream. He saw himself prophesying "LIVE!" to a dead person in a large casket. Each time he expected a resurrection. Yet each time, nothing happened.

Immediately when he shared the dream, I entered into a vision of the casket dream that the pastor was dreaming. What he saw, by the Spirit of God I somehow saw myself. Suddenly the hand of the Lord came to the casket and thrust it open. As with Lazarus, resurrection came.

God's very hand pulled out what looked to be an Egyptian mummy. Slowly and carefully this hand began to unwrap the grave clothes, beginning at the top. When the white bands were removed below the eyes, I saw that it was a woman. And as the cloths were removed from around her chest, to my astonishment there was a baby nestled in her bosom.

I knew immediately the woman represented the Bride of Christ in the nation. And not only did the Lord resurrect the bride, but also the child—the covenantal heritage of the Bridegroom and His Bride!

Immediately I heard these words: *Where you have felt like a widow, abandoned by Me and far from My hand of provision, instead I am bringing you into a season of intimacy with Me, and abundance from My hand, and indeed I have saved the best wine for last!*

Friends, we have not moved past the expiration date of this vision. In fact, it's for this very time. The Lord is clearly after our children. He is also clearly moving to secure the preservation and perpetuation of our covenantal heritage.

He is the God of the turnaround. And He will be faithful to bring it His way, for His glory. With the best wine saved for last!

But to gain this new birth of freedom, all that holds the bride and her child in the casket must be overcome. Covenant with death and hell annulled (see Isa. 28:14-15). We must fully shift from a covenant with death empowering a culture of death to a covenant of life empowering a culture of life.

Psalm 91—Security from the Secret Place

Let's now take a look at Psalm 91, highlighted to Dutch Sheets through his wife Ceci's vision. Maybe you feel uncovered or violated by the actions of others against you. Trust me that God's heart is moved by your challenges, and He wants to grant you protection. It's time to dwell in the secret place of the Most High, abiding under the shadow of the Almighty, receiving the protection He alone can give.

Psalm 91 is a great passage of Scripture to pray through. Especially given the scope of COVID-19 challenges, it is so relevant to today. Psalm 91 promises God's deliverance from both the snares of the hunters and from the deadly pestilence.

The potential for God's promised deliverance from deadly pestilence is easy to grasp, especially in this hour. And His deliverance is no more needed than now as we pray for a cessation to surges by evolving variants.

But most Christians are naively unaware of their urgent need for deliverance from the trapper. Trappers or hunters in this context hunt people as prey. They can even be compared to snipers. And their traps

> Christians are naively unaware of their urgent need for deliverance from the trapper. Trappers or hunters in this context hunt people as prey.

are often personalized. Strategies are implemented to capitalize on vulnerabilities. A "friend" assigned to seduce a pastor, a politician, or a business leader steps out of the shadows and into the family circle. A trafficker feeds a young teenager another form of "candy." Or terrorists prey upon airline security vulnerabilities to hijack planes and take down the symbols of American strength.

Here's something to ponder: The psalmist correlated deliverance from the trapper with deliverance from pestilence. Could there be a correlation? Could an engineered virus be used as an assassin's ammunition? It definitely warrants prayer.

Note that the spiritual realm parallels the natural. Many in the occult target individuals, families, and ministries through primarily spiritual means. They target government leaders. They target Kingdom projects. Their purpose is the same. Either to neutralize, exploit, leverage, or take people down to advance their dark agenda.

And most often the first thing the enemy targets is your prayer life. Why? Because a wonderful byproduct of a flourishing relationship with the Lord is the protection promised in Psalm 91. You and I choose to dwell in the secret place of the Most High. His shadow covers us. His angelic hosts are released to have charge over us. Direction becomes clear. Discernment of the spiritual realm organically matures. And the Kingdom genuinely advances.

I have learned to contend in the spirit for my prayer life as though I were fighting for the life of my child. The hardest thing is to recognize when this aspect of your life is under assault. Because the dullness that comes causes a lack of desire for the Lord. We often become introspective, assuming the hand of the Lord has lifted due to some private fault or offense.

Which may be true. If so, simply seek forgiveness. But most of the time, the enemy simply wants to disconnect you from your Source of true life. Seek God's forgiveness where needed. Call 911 and ask the Lord for help. Then pray over your prayer life, taking authority in the spirit as you would in praying for your child or friend.

And pray Psalm 91! We encourage you to pray these verses daily as well as receiving daily communion.

Amos 9:11—Restoring the Covenant Covering

*"In that day I will restore the fallen tabernacle of David...
and repair its breaches"* (Amos 9:11).

Call 911! Amid the rubble and ruin of that historic day, God's trumpet was globally sounded for the restoration of the Tabernacle of David through 24-7 worship and prayer. Both the heart and structure for God to tabernacle with us are now in place. In this era we are now securing the next phase of His restoration movement.

Amos 9:11 conveys a picture of the corporate covering that Psalm 91 promises on a personal level. Amid the challenges of today, the alarm is once again sounding from Amos 9:11 to rebuild the fallen Tabernacle of David, and repair its breaches. God desires to restore His covenant covering over America!

King David is famous for pitching a tent and launching 24-7 movement of worship and intercession. But this narrative generally neglects the reason for which the tabernacle was actually erected. From the beginning it was meant to be a dwelling place for the Ark of the Covenant.

And before David ever pitched a tent or hired worshipers, he first rescued the Ark of the Covenant from captivity. He restored the Ark back in to Israel, and afforded it the most prominent place in his capitol city. In our terms today, *by restoring the Ark, David restored his nation's covenant with God.* He brought his nation back into alignment with her covenantal foundations—spiritually, culturally, and governmentally.

When David accomplished this, a tent of covering went up. But more than this tent, the glory of God became a tangible covering over the entire land. And as a nation literally "under God," Israel was ushered into an unprecedented season of prosperity, cultural advancement, innovation, and victory over her enemies.

In short, the manifestation of Psalm 91 on a corporate level. That's what I call a turnaround!

Here's a word from the Lord for you. A storm is coming. It is similar to 9-11. It is best to get the tent of covering up before the storm hits!

> Here's a word from the Lord for you. A storm is coming. It is similar to 9-11. It is best to get the tent of covering up before the storm hits!

I want to say as well, the most personally sacred covenant covering remains a mother's womb. To the extent a nation violates this covering, the covering of the land will ultimately suffer loss. And to the extent a nation moves to restore this sacred covering, the covering of the nation will be restored. In this regard, recent Supreme Court verdicts have brought a key realignment that is absolutely vital to securing God's covering. Prophesy His restoration!

Their time is now ours. The principle remains the same. Our realignment with God's covenant is advancing on all fronts. It's now time to recover our covenant covering!

> *"On that day I will raise up the fallen tabernacle of David, and wall up its gaps; I will also raise up its ruins and rebuild it as in the days of old"* (Amos 9:11).

> *"When the Lord has washed away the filth of the daughters of Zion and purged the bloodshed of Jerusalem from her midst, by the spirit of judgment and the spirit of burning, then the Lord will create over the entire area of Mount Zion and over her assemblies a cloud by day, and smoke, and the brightness of a flaming fire by night; for over all the glory will be a (bridal) canopy"* (Isaiah 4:4-5).

The Experts Are Needed

Let's draw a final lesson from the "Call 911" warning dream. As we have shared, amid the state of emergency the Lord wants to bring our nation into what Abraham Lincoln described as "a new birth of freedom." An awakening. A turnaround, yielding to Him.

We are once again in a season of intense travail as the Body of Christ. This travail is to bring to birth the next season of Kingdom advancement. A new birth of freedom. God is releasing His turnaround decrees to define this new era His way.

Yet just as Ceci's dream predicted in the hours before 9-11-01, America's response to both the crisis and the potential for blessing was by no means adequate. Twenty years after the awakening alarm was sounded,

America has still largely failed to fully turn. Meanwhile, the child, representing America's new birth of freedom, remains extremely vulnerable.

Maybe these backstories will help you more fully appreciate the weight of what Jolene and I are conveying. We are in a midnight hour. On a national level, this time the midnight turnaround must genuinely be secured. Covenant, life, and awakening must prevail. Freedom must prevail.

You are being equipped as an expert for your time. An Eliakim. I pray you sense the passion behind God's clear invitation for you to respond. Because in a very real way the future of our nation depends on it.

Turnaround Decree 5:
The 911 Decree—Securing God's Protective Covering

By Jon & Jolene Hamill with Tom Harlow, special forces, retired.

> *WE THE PEOPLE OF GOD do fully and voluntarily choose to dwell in Your secret place, Most High, and station ourselves to abide under Your shadow, God the Almighty. We declare that You are our refuge and our fortress, our God in whom we wholeheartedly put our trust.*
>
> *We proclaim the decree of the Lord. Surely You deliver us from the snares and traps of the hunter! We affirm Your deliverance from all trappers, hunters, occult watchers, etc., as well as all associated traps, ambushes, and any weapons fabricated to harm, impede, or deter us from our destiny in You. Keep us hidden from their eyes, in both the spiritual and natural realms. Expose any and all enemies now hidden in our midst and deliver us from their hands. We declare their tracking and targeting must now cease, and*

all eavesdropping devices must now be disempowered and nullified, in Jesus' Name.

We also declare Your deliverance from the deadly pestilences and calamities. By the power and authority of Your Word, we entrust Your protection; the destructive pestilences must be restrained from us as well as every sphere You have entrusted to our dominion. Lord, we stand still and see Your Salvation as You are NOW disempowering both the besetting plague and all demonic forces empowering them, as we come into agreement with Your Word. However and whenever the pestilence has taken hold, we affirm it must dis-integrate and be removed without any further residual or harmful effects to the body. We declare full restoration— spirit, soul, and body, in Jesus' Name.

And where maligned humanistic or spiritual entities have in any way been targeting us or our families, including through the use of chemical, biological, or malicious spiritual weapons, we declare in the Name of Jesus, that they will now to be exposed and restrained from accomplishing their vile deeds.

Preserve our lives! And bring Your retaliation against the wicked, for Your glory.

Bring us now into synergy with the move of Your Spirit and the angelic hosts of the Lord Jesus Christ. We decree that Your angels are now released to have charge over us, to watch over us, keep us, protect and defend us in all our ways. Therefore we tread upon the lion, the cobra, the serpent, including the demonic entities symbolically represented. We thank You that You have granted us authority to tread upon serpents and scorpions, and overcome all the power of the *enemy, so that nothing shall by any means harm us (Luke 10:19).*

Lord Almighty, El Shaddai, because You love us, and we love You, You will save us. You now set us securely on high, because we have known know Your names, the names conveying Your Character, Power, and Glory. You will hear us as we call on You; You will be with us in trouble. You rescue us and honor us, and with long life You will satisfy us and show us Your salvation!

And Lord for the United States of America, as covenant with You has been restored as validated by Heaven's Court, we come into agreement with You and decree that You now restore Your covenant covering from region to region. We decree this covering is now extended over the White House, the Capitol, the Supreme Court, and all extensions of these three branches of our government, over our military, diplomatic and intelligence communities, both here and abroad, and over our economic capacities.

Lord, restore Your glory! We declare that Holy Spirit now becomes the spiritual undercurrent and overarching influence of our land, dispossessing all other powers. Concurrent with the restoration of Your covenant covering, we say You are now releasing the next phase of Your Amos 9:11 restoration. Grace Your people to now establish perpetual worship to Yu that releases the atmosphere of Heaven into our spheres.

And we now decree Your anointing to possess and establish Your covenantal inheritance in this land.

And as You promised protection from all our enemies according to Your covenant (2 Kings 17:38-39), we now release the hand of the Lord to bring deliverance from the hands and weapons of all adversaries of Your covenant, both foreign and domestic. We declare Your protection and deliverance over all our gates, including all our ports. We declare that You now restore America's gatekeeping capacities while protecting and preserving our foundational freedoms.

In Jesus' Name, and for Your glory! AMEN.

SEVEN ON A SCROLL:
Characteristics of Eliakim

God's Eliakims are among the experts needed for our time. Remember, the primary qualification is a dedication to be a father and mother to your family and sphere. Our calling today is not just to pray for Eliakims, but to become Elikaims. Here are seven characteristics of Eliakim:

1. Loves God.

2. Loves spiritual children and natural children. Devoted to parenting. Devoted to others besides self!

3. Responsible. Honest, dependable, trustworthy as a lifestyle.

4. Stable provider.

5. Gained competence to excel in field and lead well.

6. Honors parents—mentored and mentoring.

7. Builds wisely on legacy.

CHAPTER 6

THE MIDNIGHT TURNAROUND

"In the year of King Uzziah's death I saw the Lord sitting on a throne" (Isaiah 6:1).

HEAVEN'S DIRECTION OFTEN BECOMES CLEAR in the midst of a crisis. It is as though an alarm sounds to awaken us both to the challenges we face, and the potential for the turnaround God is offering us to define our future. Our nation was birthed out of one such awakening alarm. And it catalyzed one of the greatest turning points in the history of global freedom.

In a midnight hour, a distant relative of mine named Paul Revere was alerted to an immediate invasion by British troops by signals from a church tower. He rode through the night from city to city, sounding the alarm to awaken an army. A midnight cry during a midnight ride! Revere's efforts started a revolution, securing a turnaround for freedom.

A year later the 13 Colonies banded together in Philadelphia to write the turnaround decree called the Declaration of Independence. And a new era began.

Cindy Jacobs once prophesied that Jolene and I would carry a similar forerunning call to Paul Revere. Holding out a burning lamp and riding from city to city, we would resound an awakening alarm. Within this alarm vision for the future would also be released. Awakening. Turnaround. Freedom. The Lord is coming!

As we mentioned in chapter 1, peering out our window to Washington, DC, back in 2017, Holy Spirit began to unfold clear revelation of the midnight cry of our time: *By the year 2020 there will be a series of midnight crises. How the Body of Christ confronts these crises, and overcomes them, will even become a roadmap for believers living in the final hours of the end times.*

Matthew 25 was highlighted as the roadmap. A midnight crisis where multitudes would fall into slumber while the Lord delays His intervention. A midnight cry from a remnant of watchmen who remained awake. And a midnight turnaround as a new movement breaks forth, and His direct intervention becomes released. No more delay!

As we've chronicled, recent events seemed to confirm the warning of a midnight hour. A global pandemic. Manufactured disinformation fueled by elites within government and media, intended to take down the president of the United States. A defective election. The overturning of godly laws. It seemed the hand of God had lifted, and to an extent evil was no longer restrained.

We've been in a midnight hour. And the Spirit bears witness. Around the 20th anniversary of September 11, our prophetic friend Lynnie Harlow was given an incredible experience. We posted the word immediately. In her own words:

> I saw a clock and knew in my dream it was the clock over this Nation (it was a time gate). I noticed it was one minute until 12:00 a.m. but the long handle got stuck and so it just keep clicking in place at one minute to midnight. I watched it for a bit and finally it clicked one more time and was unstuck and the clock rang "12:00!" When it did there was a violent earthquake here in the DC and I knew we had just crossed a threshold.
>
> I felt like the handle that was stuck was being held back by God. When it was HIS kairos moment... He let it go and the clock

struck 12:00. Again, this was a TIME GATE and I knew we had just crossed a threshold.

Friends, God is giving clarity on the time in which we live. We are no longer close to a midnight hour. Now we are in a midnight hour. The good news is that a midnight turnaround—with a great awakening—is now on the way. The pages ahead will frame it out for you to access its transforming power.

A major reason why *Turnaround Decrees* is being released at this time is to help lay the tracks for this midnight turnaround. Because it's "now" time. The season of His intervention is here. And what the enemy meant for evil is going to be turned for good.

"In the Year King Uzziah Died I Saw the Lord"

The role of prophetic watchmen is similar to their counterparts in the intelligence community. A major aspect of a watchman's job is to accurately convey accurate intelligence. If either side of the equation is missing— if accurate intelligence is exaggerated when it is shared, or if the intelligence conveyed is inaccurate—a disaster is set in motion.

It's like when your eyes see distortions of what is really there. Which in my view occurred with so many prophetic expressions surrounding the

> Prophecy: By the year 2020 there will be a series of midnight crises. How the Body of Christ confronts these crises, and overcomes them, will even become a roadmap for believers living in the final hours of the end times.

2020 elections. Visions, dreams, and words were shared. Decrees were made. But something unperceived was not being dealt with.

People ask me if I saw prophetically the election results. The answer is yes—reservedly. In May 2019 I saw Donald Trump being shifted from the presidency in a way that would shake the nation to its core. The last chapter of our book *White House Watchmen* actually deals with this, though in deliberately veiled terms. From Isaiah 6:1: *"In the year King Uzziah died I saw the Lord seated on a throne, lofty and exalted, with the train of His robe filling the temple."*

When the Spirit of God showed this to me, I actually feared President Trump could be assassinated. The other alternative, which in the end proved true, was that he might lose the upcoming election.

It was in Jerusalem, on May 20, 2019, that the Lord visited me over this passage. Jolene and I were preparing for the evening meeting at Succat Hallel, a 24-7 prayer center founded by dear friends Rick and Patricia Ridings. Similar to our watchman's perch overlooking Washington, DC, Succat Hallel has a breathtaking view of Mount Zion and the Temple Mount. The Lord identifies this geographic area alone as the center of His throne on earth.

As I read through Isaiah 6, I suddenly realized that it was on this mount—identified as His very throne—that the prophet Isaiah encountered the Lord. The gateposts of a literal temple shook as the governmental glory of God crossed the threshold. The Temple was filled with the substance of Heaven. And Isaiah saw the Lord!

The overall context is Israel was ushered into a time of governmental shaking where a beloved king named Uzziah was unseated. Within a year of the suffered loss, Isaiah was visited. I knew immediately a very difficult season was coming to America through a transition in America's highest office. I saw the same for Israel, and for the United Kingdom.

We also knew God's response in the midst would be to usher us all, including these three nations, into a season of visitation that defines our future.

A "Call 911" moment immediately followed the release of this word. In Israel, Prime Minister Netanyahu was unable to form the coalition necessary to establish a new government. New elections were called. Jolene and I then flew to from Jerusalem to London to continue our ministry tour. And on May 23, just four days after the Lord spoke to me from this passage, UK Prime Minister Theresa May unexpectedly resigned.

I knew the scope was global. But what I did not fully grasp is how virtually every person in the globe would soon suffer the grief of loss from the COVID crisis.

The good news accompanying this prophetic warning is that as in the days of Isaiah, the Lord is now going to begin to unveil His unshakeable throne. His governmental glory is moving through our gates. As with Isaiah, many will become undone by their encounters with Him. The awe of God, and respect for His majesty, will be restored. An anointing of holy conviction will again penetrate hardened hearts. This conviction will be restored to both church and government.

> Prophecy: as in the days of Isaiah, the Lord is now going to begin to unveil His unshakeable throne. His governmental glory is moving through our gates. As with Isaiah, many will become undone by their encounters with Him. The awe of God, and respect for His majesty, will be restored.

We together will see the depths to which we have sunk in our selfish pursuits. A tremendous cleansing has actually begun. Eventually the suffered loss will even become a catalyst for what can only be called a midnight turnaround.

Purging the Prophetic—Isaiah's Internal Turnaround

The Bible records that Isaiah served as King Uzziah's intercessor and prophet. He served the king for many years, and was heavily invested in his success. I bet you can imagine what it must have felt like for Isaiah when Uzziah's kingship was removed. Probably similar to many of you reading this after praying so hard through the 2020 elections.

In the midst of this shaking, Isaiah saw the Lord seated on His throne. The prophet was, in his own words, undone. There was a dimension of glory unveiled in which his own sinful condition became clear.

Remember, Isaiah was the highest-level prophet in Israel. He's the guy you would want to invite to secure big crowds for your conferences or your prayer calls.

"I am a man of unclean lips!" Isaiah cried. "And I dwell in the midst of a people of unclean lips!"

God responded with coals of fire to cleanse him. In a similar manner, we and many other prophets, intercessors, and leaders today are embracing a new level of purging directly from the heart of God. Just as with Isaiah, a primary issue God is showing us is the condition of our own mouths.

In a recent vision I found myself in a dentist's office. Somehow I was watching the appointment unfold from inside the back of my mouth. Quite a view!

Immediately an elderly gray-haired dentist approached me, wearing a bright headlamp. He shined his light in my mouth. I opened my mouth wide for him to examine.

The dentist put his hand to my mouth, an instrument in his hand. I was expecting a tongue depressor. But instead he held a plumb line to my mouth, examining it intently. The disease he was searching for was deception. He looked at me, nodded, and simply said, "Passed."

The dentist then stood up and moved to the next patient. The process was gentle but absolutely clinical and unbiased.

Immediately by the Spirit I saw how the Lord was now examining His prophets across the nation. The plumb line for God's evaluation comes from 1 Peter 2:22. *"He committed no sin, nor was any deceit found in his mouth."* What a description of our Messiah! Even in his journey to the cross, Jesus never wavered. He never compromised. No false words ever escaped His mouth to try and influence others, validate His legitimacy or gifting, or to spare him from the trial at hand.

Can I ask you: Has intentional deceit been found in your mouth? How about malice or slander? Unforgiveness? Betrayal? Are you greedy, as the apostle Peter warned, exploiting others through false words? (see 2 Pet. 2:3) The Lord is issuing this warning to all of us. He wants to purify the mouths of His people so He in turn can bring greater revelation and warnings through you.

Just like Isaiah's coals of fire, the purging might be temporarily painful. Sometimes you even feel more undone afterward than before. That's because God's purging cleanses us at a root level from the things we are repenting over, in the hidden places of our heart or even our in generational line. It is amazing how often these roots are tied directly to our identity.

The good news is that through the process, you and I are being recalibrated with a new level of intimacy, genuineness, accuracy, and authority the Lord desires to grant, and you desire to embody.

That's because God's purging cleanses us at a root level from the things we are repenting over. The good news is that through the process, you and I are being recalibrated with a new level of intimacy, genuineness, accuracy, and authority the Lord desires to grant, and you desire to embody.

It's no coincidence that Isaiah began decreeing the genuine word of the Lord soon after his purging. This cannot be emphasized enough. Isaiah's cleansing was necessary for him to release throne room scrolls that were not compromised by personal or political bias. Because he gained cleansing at a higher level, he was able to decree from a higher level. And so will you.

Look at the authority entrusted to the prophet. He decreed the birth of Messiah from a virgin. He decreed the ever-expanding governance of the nations on Messiah's shoulders. He saw and decreed Messiah's suffering for all mankind, followed by His resurrection and eternal reign. He prophesied Israel's rebirth. And he prophesied the burning lamps that would one day secure Israel's restoration as a nation married to the Lord!

God is fashioning you the same way, even through the fire.

Let's review our key principles to better understand our progression so far. Covenant with God becomes the foundation for the turnaround you are seeking. Repentance brings the realignment necessary for His covenant blessing to be manifested. Then finally, God's purging brings an internal cleansing, an internal turnaround which is vitally necessary for you to decree and steward His external turnarounds in your world.

Take the coals, cleanse my lips, here I am!

Jon's Midnight Purging

Talk about the need for cleansing. Jolene and I had just evacuated Washington, DC, for a much-needed time of recuperation following Inauguration Day 2021. The word of the Lord to us was literally "Detox from DC."

I remember pouring my heart out to Him on our way down I-95 toward our Georgia destination. Two questions predominated: First, *Do You still want us in Washington, DC? Should we still remain?* And second, *Is a national Glory Train journey still on Your heart?* Because with all that just transpired, I would figure we should expect Ichabod, or "glory departed," rather than the restoration of His glory in our nation. The Great Withdrawal, not the Great Awakening!

My grieving heart demanded indulgence from the moment we got to Georgia. We slept in. We ate very full meals. We failed to refuse very full desserts, especially when peaches and cobbler were both in the equation. I don't know if you've ever tried to overcome your grief with food before. Let's just say the results are both limited and expansive at the same time.

Meanwhile, God was seemingly leaving me alone. For a time I almost preferred it that way.

On February 9, I awoke at exactly 4:00 in the morning to a very humbling dream. In the dream I was slumbering through an ordained time of prayer. Crumbs of food were on my quilted blanket, left over from a recent midnight snack. Meanwhile, it seemed like Holy Spirit was at a great distance. As if I could not find Him.

I have to say, all aspects were honest and accurate.

Suddenly I was given an invitation to minister at the International House of Prayer in Kansas City. I raced through the Bible, hoping to find passages to share. Psalm 110, Isaiah 40, and Isaiah 55 were all highlighted. They were all very familiar. But I could not even find the passages because clippings from newspaper stories were stuffed between the pages.

The dream brought me face-to-face with my reality. Prayer had given way to sleep. Comfort food had become my diet at all hours. And countless times my devotional reading had succumbed to scouring for news updates on my phone or laptop.

Basically, it took a dream from the Lord to realize how significantly my own self-indulgence, connected to grief, was hindering my relationship with the Lord. This might be an area for you to explore more as well.

As I awoke, the Lord spoke to me simply, *Come up higher.*

This dream started a series of 4 a.m. prayer encounters. For the first time in months, getting out of bed for early morning prayer was both easy and a delight. The times were rich with presence. Revelation flowed. I read the Bible with renewed passion.

In the midst, the Lord began to deal with pent-up anger. Especially over squandered opportunities by certain officials when the destiny of our nation was on the line. Entire mornings were spent forgiving both people and institutions I felt had ultimately betrayed His intentions. Finally, a heaviness of grief I had carried through the most of the election season lifted. My spirit felt buoyant again. Though I didn't experience living coals from Heaven like Isaiah, I knew a significant purging of my life had been completed.

And once more a hunger for the Lord overtook desire for the regional cuisine.

If you can identify with my scenario, the Lord is present with you to regain lost ground. Each circumstance will be different. So will your pathway forward. But if you ask Him to help, I guarantee He will be there for you!

Turnaround! From Isaiah 53 to Isaiah 54

In the midst of this season of renewal, the Lord spoke to me a very clear word which was for both you and me personally and for the nation. I cannot explain it any other way than to say that it came as a revelatory "flash."

I knew immediately the year 2020 could only be understood through the lens of Isaiah 53. Further, I knew He was shifting us into a new season and a new dimension, defined by Isaiah 54.

You and this nation have been in a season of Isaiah 53, where the arm of the Lord seemed restrained and My people seemed forsaken. In time you will understand my covenant purposes, because hindsight will indeed become 2020.

But as of March 4 I am bringing you and the nation into a season defined by Isaiah 54, where the hand of the Lord returns to His Bride. In your seeming barrenness it is time to sing again! It's time to step out in faith and enlarge the place of your tent. You will break out to the right and to the left. Your seed will possess the nations. All your children will be taught of the Lord. No weapon forged against you will prosper. My covenant with you, and with this nation, remains secure!

Note that Isaiah 53 portrays Jesus as the suffering servant in His crucifixion. *"Who has believed our report, and to whom has the hand of the Lord been revealed?,"* the text begins. Isaiah then begins to prophesy about how Israel's Messiah will be wounded for our transgressions and bruised for our iniquities, with the punishment which brings us peace being laid on Him.

Jesus fulfilled this Scripture down to the last terrifying detail. The "Hand of the Lord"—of Jesus Himself—was willingly, brutally restrained for a moment, nailed to a wooden cross.

We know now that Messiah's suffering to secure our eternal redemption. But imagine what it was like for the followers of Jesus at the time, watching as their Redeemer suffered in agony. Despair and fear must have flooded their hearts. Love was crucified. Hope died. Israel's long-promised Redeemer had succumbed to the brutal torture of the Romans. In a very real way, it seemed that the global government of their hour had prevailed over their long-promised Messiah.

Given that hindsight is 2020, maybe you see a few parallels to the unimaginable year we finally exited. With all certainty I can say the hand of the Lord had been restrained from acting. It looked as though an evil global governmental structure had won.

And just as Jesus Christ appeared completely defeated at the very time He was securing our redemption, so in 2020, the time of our greatest seeming defeat was actually the very moment our covenant restoration with Messiah took place. Remember the Mayflower Covenant Renewal. Four hundred years exactly from the time our nation was consecrated to Him by the Pilgrims, our covenant renewal with Christ was secured. This occurred one week precisely after the election. And this generational covenant with the Lord will in the end set the course for the future.

I'm going to prophesy to you:

Messiah prevailed to redeem us by His covenant. So, too, will He prevail through this covenant restoration to give us all a window for redemption and turnaround. This turnaround movement will absolutely affect the highest halls of government. But it's different from the previous expression. This time around the covenantal turnarounds are much broader in scope, focused first on your own life, then your home and family. These are the priorities reflected in Isaiah 54. And they are essential to secure enduring national turnaround.

No King but Jesus!

Isaiah 54: the Hand of the Lord Returns

In Isaiah 54 the countenance of God turns back to the Bride. The hand of God returns to the Bride. And prophetically, when she holds His hand again, pressed against His eternal scars, the depth of His redemption begins to dawn on her in an overwhelming way.

Let's start with the first verse. I like the Complete Jewish Study Bible translation the best.

> *"Sing o barren woman! Burst into song, shout with joy; for the deserted wife will have more children than the woman who is living with her husband, says Adonai."*

Note this whole passage is a love letter to the deserted bride. It is also a contract with her and a decree for her.

Through 2020, in the face of COVID, national polarization, election dysfunction, and so much more, it seemed to many as though the Lord had deserted His people. Our most

> This time around the covenantal turnarounds are much broader in scope, focused first on your own life, then your home and family. These are the priorities reflected in Isaiah 54. And they are essential to secure enduring national turnaround.

substantive prayers seemed completely barren, conceiving no victory and birthing no miracle. As Hezekiah observed, the children had come to term, and truly there was no strength to deliver.

But in this new season, God Himself is breaking barrenness and securing the fruit of our efforts. So much so that we will have to enlarge our capacities! I believe He is first referring to our intimacy with Him, and the overflow that comes from the womb of our spirit through prayer. Everything else follows from this stream.

> *"Enlarge the space for your tent; extend the curtains of your dwelling, do not hold back; lengthen your cords and make your tent pegs firm. For you will spread out to the right and to the left. And your descendants will possess the nations and will resettle the desolate cities!"* (Isa. 54:2-3).

Watch this now. Where many of you felt abandoned, almost like a widow, the Lord is saying your covenant with Him remains secure. Your Maker is your Husband!

> *Don't be afraid, for you won't be ashamed... You will forget the shame of your youth, no longer remember the dishonor of being widowed. For your husband is your Maker, Adonai-Tz- va'ot (the Lord of Hosts) is his name. The Holy One of Isra'el is your Redeemer. He will be called the God of all the earth. For Adonai has called you back like a wife abandoned and grief-striken;... "Briefly I abandoned you, but with great com- passion I am taking you back. I was angry for a moment and hid my face from you; but with everlasting grace I will have compassion on you," says Adonai your Redeemer. "For me this is like Noach's flood. Just as I swore that no flood like Noach's would ever again cover the earth, so now I swear that I will*

never be angry with you or rebuke you... My grace will never leave you, and my covenant of peace will not be removed."... No weapon made will prevail against you (verses 4-10, 17).

Isaiah 54 Turnaround—Two Confirmations

How the Lord confirmed this transition into Isaiah 54 is astonishing. As we've shared, Jolene and I set our hearts to seek the Lord in late January. We disengaged from all ministry obligations and headed to Georgia, our hearts full of questions. *How do you want us to invest our lives in the coming season? Given the circumstances, should we remain in DC or is this aspect of our calling over? And what about the Glory Train?*

I had long sensed the Lord saying a fresh Glory Train journey was at hand for 2021, similar in magnitude to 2016. Before the election it made sense. From Inauguration Day on, when executive orders were enacted in clear defiance of God's heart and word, it made no sense. So much of what we had labored for had seemingly been reversed.

The Railroad Key

Right around February 2, as we were beginning our "detox time" in Georgia, a key arrived in a package. The Lord had told our friends Russ and Julie to send us a "railroad key"! This small key unlocked the potential to *change the trajectory of the tracks!* And I knew the Lord was unlocking covenantal authority to even to change the trajectory of the nation. Turnaround!

Note that we had not shared what we were sensing for a fresh Glory Train tour with anyone. The railroad key confirmed this project in an extraordinary way.

The Washington Key

Toward the end of our "detox time" seeking the Lord, after He had shown us the turnaround from Isaiah 53 to 54, our friend Lauren Main connected with us. She wanted to present us with a few special gifts in her hometown of Jacksonville, Florida.

And she chose Purim for the time of this presentation. First, we were presented with a plaque with a golden gavel. The gavel represented Heaven's affirmation of the Mayflower Covenant Renewal.

And we were presented with yet another key. It is a replica of the "Mount Vernon key" given to George Washington, known as the father of our nation, in commemoration of his courageous stand for freedom. The original key is on display Mount Vernon.

Washington was born, by the way, on 2-22. Remember how Eliakim was given the key of David, as shared in Isaiah 22:22. Eliakim was called as a "father to the house of Judah and the inhabitants of Jerusalem." Lauren felt to prophetically convey that God is establishing us a father and mother to the nation and the capitol city. Incredible confirmation to remain in Washington, DC!

And both keys confirmed the Isaiah 54 turnaround. Lengthen your cords, strengthen your stakes. You're going to break forth to the right and the left. Time to step out in faith!

Alaska! The Isaiah 54 Turnaround

With this at heart, we decided to launch the 50 state Glory Train tour over Passover 2021. Let My people go! Chris Mitchell, Jr. decided to join Jolene and me for the entire project.

In 2016 we started our 50-state tour from the tropical paradise of Hawaii. But after much prayer, the Lord strongly highlighted Alaska as the destination to launch the Glory Train 2021. As we were preparing, friends sent us many prophetic words about the state. A word from Chuck Pierce hit me like a freight train: "Alaska is a gateway of the Ancient of Days!"

Ancient of Days.

There's only one chapter in the Bible that refers to God in this way: Daniel 7. The chapter that chronicles the Dan. 7:22 Turnaround verdict. To me it was confirmation that God's turnaround was being released.

Not coincidentally our first stop was in the Alaskan town of Homer. It is affectionately known as the "end of the road" because it is the westernmost point on the US highway system. And for whatever reason, the Lord brought us to the "end of the road" for America to governmentally decree this turnaround!

In Homer we began sharing on the ultimate Passover miracle, Christ's redemption, and resurrection. It was a perfect segue to prophesy the national shift from Isaiah 53 to 54.

And over Passover 2021, the "Isaiah 54 Turnaround" was first governmentally decreed from the end of the road to the nation.

Shoshana's Story

I have to mention a new friend who shuttled Jolene and me around. To protect her privacy let's call her Shoshana. During a five-hour road trip from Palmer to the "end of the road," Shoshana asked us for a preview of what the Lord was saying. A loaded question for sure, but we had plenty of time. When I mentioned the shift from Isaiah 53 to 54, her eyes began to well up with tears.

It turns out that in 2020 our new friend Shoshana had been abandoned by her husband. In her own words:

My then-husband and I were building a home together. I had even pulled out retirement funds to invest in it. But less than 10 days after we moved in, over Passover 2020, he suddenly threw my daughter and me out. It was violent and completely unexpected.

He then began to stalk us—breaking into my office and my car.

So in the height of the pandemic, we had lost our home, food, toiletries, medications, and even my daughter's school supplies. We literally only had the clothes on our back and our purses. With my extended family locked down, I couldn't even go to them. I didn't know where to go or what to do. But we needed to escape.

Out of nowhere a friend called, and when I shared about our plight, she graciously offered an apartment to us. It was furnished and even had two rolls of toilet paper. I cried. I was able to get together some groceries and we hid there for about a month. My former husband served me with divorce papers, and when I responded he finally began to leave us alone.

All I could do is cling to the Lord. One time in prayer He focused me on Isaiah 54. Surrounded by barrenness, despair, and rejection I identified immediately with the agony portrayed in the passage. Then I heard the Lord say, "Sing o barren one." And the Lord Himself made seemingly impossible promises real to me. Worshiping through my pain was hard at first. I sang and waited, cried and sang, clinging to His promises over and over. My journal entries became covered in tears. O tempest-tossed woman, I will lay your foundations with sapphires.

Shoshana's story does not end there though. Abandoned by her husband in the middle of a pandemic, she and her daughter began to experience miraculous intervention from God's hand. That's the only way to describe it. First on the docket was a purchase of a new home—built from scratch and secured just before the supply and labor shortages caused prices to skyrocket.

During construction, Shoshana inscribed passages from Isaiah 54 on all the frames and doorposts. "The Lord told me to expand my tent and I obeyed," she simply explained.

And the bills have always been paid. "I still don't know how it happens each month, and don't know how the next month will be provided for, but I am His Bride and He is my Husband and we are safe under His covering. So I keep singing, working hard and following His lead!"

Note that it was on Passover 2021, exactly one year after Shoshana and her daughter were pushed out by an abusive husband, that she volunteered to drive Jolene and me to Homer. She asked Jolene and me what we were hearing from the Lord. Isaiah 54 was the reply that began our conversation. And suddenly it became only fitting that we were driving to the end of the road to proclaim God's Isaiah 54 turnaround for the nation.

Oh. Did I mention that Shoshana received her verdict of divorce from her abusive husband on 7-22-2020? Remember Daniel 7:22. On this date in a remote town in Alaska judgment was rendered in favor of His saints within only three months of the horrific betrayal she suffered.

Can't make this stuff up. For real.

Turnarounds for Your House and Sphere!

In a very real way, our friend Shoshana became a sign of the Isaiah 54 turnaround He is bringing for all of us. Again, these turnarounds are coming covenantally to the nation. But most importantly, they are coming, at your invitation, to your own house! I'm prophesying to you here. By this Isaiah 54 movement the Body of Christ will be purified, enriched, and built up *from the inside out*.

Rainbow over US Capitol, April 2021, confirming Isaiah 54. Photo: Jon Hamill

Maybe it's only appropriate that the decree below was actually written by Shoshana. We encourage you to engage with it from the heart, and claim the promises He is offering as your own.

Can I share just one final confirmation of this Isaiah 54 turnaround? A few days after we returned from Alaska, I stepped out on our watchman's perch and saw this incredible scene of a rainbow over Washington, DC. The rainbow literally formed in our back area, then crossed over the Potomac River to encompass the US Capitol. A picture is worth a thousand words. From Alaska to DC, His covenant prevails!

From Isaiah 54: *"For Me this is like Noah's flood. Just as I swore that no flood like Noah's would ever again cover the earth, so now I swear that I will never be angry with you or rebuke you.... My grace will never leave you, and my covenant of peace will not be removed."*

Turnaround Decree 6:
The Isaiah 54 Decree—Contract with the Bride

By Shoshana

> *WE THE BRIDE, being of sound mind do fully and voluntary agree and declare that that there is No King but Jesus Christ! And we position ourselves within the covering of our Bridegroom and Kinsmen Redeemer. I (insert name) ask for, and align myself within, the Restorative Redemption of my Creator. As defined in the following terms:*
>
> *Parties: Creator of the Universe (HUSBAND), believer (BRIDE)*
>
> *Terms: Defining actions from the Bride and promises activated by God in response to actions in keeping with His covenant.*

Actions for God's people:

1. Sing O Barren Woman! Return to worship and gratitude, you who have not borne. "Burst into song, shout for joy you who have never been in labor; for more are the children of the desolate woman than the children of the married wife."

2. Enlarge the place of your tent and stretch your tent curtains wide. Do not hold back. Lengthen your cords, strengthen your stakes. Take action to possess your covenant promise!

3. Do not be afraid. Do not fear disgrace. Replace fear with faith in God's integrity to fulfill His promise to you.

PROMISES TO THE BRIDE
(concurrent with her actions of faith):

1. Favor, blessing restored. More are the children of the desolate woman than of the married woman, says the Lord. For you will spread out to the right and to the left. Your descendants will dispossess nations and restore desolate cities.

2. Covenant Restored and Affirmed. Your Maker/Creator is your Husband. The Lord Almighty is His name (reflecting His heart and character toward you). The Holy One of Israel is your Redeemer, the God of the whole earth!

3. Hand of the Lord restored. Face of the Lord restored. No longer forsaken! *"The Lord will call you back as if you were a wife deserted and distressed in spirit, who married young only to be rejected, says your God. For a brief moment I hid My face from you but with deep compassion I will bring you back."* It must be noted that the Father Himself was required to hide His face from His only begotten Son when Jesus took on Himself the sins of the world, securing our eternal redemption. Jesus is forever worthy!

4. Removal of shame. You will not be put to shame, you will not be humiliated. Through our partnership you will forget the shame of previous sin and become free from the reproach of widowhood, rejection, and abandonment.

5. Godly foundations empowered, Godly boundaries rebuilt. *"O you afflicted one, tossed with tempest, and not comforted, behold, I will lay your stones with colorful gems, and lay your foundations with sapphires. I will make your pinnacles of rubies, your gates of crystal, and all your walls of precious stones."*

6. Shalom of children—attentive care by the Lord. *"All your children shall be taught by the Lord, and great shall be the peace of your children. In righteousness you shall be established; you shall be far from oppression, for you shall not fear; and from terror, for it shall not come near you."*

7. Vindication from the Lord. *"'No weapon formed against you shall prosper, and every tongue that rises against you in judgment you shall condemn. This is the heritage of the servants of the Lord, and their righteousness and vindication are from Me,' says the Lord."*

PART 3

ANCIENT
OF DAYS

CHAPTER 7

THE TURNAROUND VERDICT

"Blessed is the nation whose God is the Lord" (Psalm 33:12).

DEEP INSIDE YOU THERE IS GREATNESS. A nobility, destiny, and purpose uniquely imparted by the very breath of your Creator. As with Shoshana, more than likely your greatness has been tenaciously opposed by the enemy. You've probably felt a measure of resistance for most of your life.

Maybe life has dealt you a difficult hand. Maybe you've been rejected or abused. Maybe you've never felt delighted in, invested in, or honored—never truly seen.

Perhaps you've even been persuaded to sell out your integrity, compromising your God-given greatness for momentary gain or pleasure. Or maybe you've done everything right. You've fought hard, but you've still been marginalized by the enemy. Sidelined for no apparent reason, except perhaps for your love for Jesus.

You haven't given up yet—but maybe you feel overwhelmed.

Wherever you are in life, you cannot fully attain your God-given potential without overcoming your adversary and redeeming what's been compromised. As you've probably already discovered, your true adversary is spiritual, and he's much stronger than you are. You cannot overcome by your strength alone.

I hope what we've shared so far is good news for you. Like the saints of old, and like many people today, you might just find that the ancient

Turnaround verdict, referenced before and explored in-depth in this chapter, becomes a key to unlocking your turnaround.

Daniel's Turnaround

The affairs of state had consumed his day, and then his night as well. So the prophet Daniel ascended to his makeshift prayer chamber, built within the upper room of his dwelling, in complete darkness. He hesitated to call the elegant residence home. That title belonged to Zion alone. The prophet had dreamed of owning a palace there someday. Or even just an apartment. Only the location truly mattered.

But by and large, Daniel had resigned himself to the solemn fact that he would never see his true home again, at least in his lifetime. Therefore his window faced east to help direct his prayers—toward Zion, toward the Temple, toward the Covenant Land.

Daniel may not get to return in his lifetime, but his prayers would. Further, he resolved that by the grace of God his people would. After 70 years of exile, restoration would begin. It had been decreed.

Passion for the Jews' return burned in his spirit from the days of his youth, the days of his own departure into Babylon. Into exile. His childhood memories of the Covenant Land had faded. But the dream had not. Over decades God's promise had remained the unyielding focus of his private intercession in this "Exile House of Prayer."

Daniel lit the candles of his menorah and placed it by the window. A welcome breeze set the flames dancing, provoking light and shadow into combat across his wall. Suddenly the Spirit of God came upon him. He saw the Lord seated on His throne. Scrolls were in his hand. An aged man of similar stature bowed low, his eyes soaked with tears. It was an unfamiliar scene from the other times he had been "there." Because nobody wept in Heaven, except for joy.

"Stop weeping!" Daniel commanded the man, his eyes becoming moistened himself. "Behold the Lion of the Tribe of Judah. He has prevailed."

How did he know this? Suddenly time stood still. In a flash his eyes beheld what his mouth was prophesying.

> *"I kept looking in the night visions," Daniel later wrote.
> "Behold, with the clouds of Heaven, One like a son of man
> was coming, and He came up to the Ancient of Days and
> was presented before Him. And to Him was given dominion, honor, and a kingdom, so that all the peoples, nations,
> and populations of all languages might serve him. His
> dominion is an everlasting dominion which will not pass
> away. And His kingdom is one which will not be destroyed!"*
> (Daniel 7:13-14).

The Precedent

Remember that your turnaround decree must be sourced from a verdict. It must be based upon Heaven's legal precedent.

Earlier in the book we explored how, in Revelation 5, the apostle John saw Jesus prevailing through His blood covenant to release Heaven's turnaround decrees. Jesus was found worthy by Heaven's Court both to rule and to open the scrolls containing the ultimate redemption of mankind. To Him dominion was literally given, or conferred. His covenant was granted the authority to unlock your destiny!

Here's a new discovery for you. And if you're like me, you will remain in a stunned state for the next few hours at least.

Because the exact same throne room scene chronicled by John is also conveyed in the book of Daniel—actually in chapter 7, the same chapter that hosts the Turnaround Verdict. Daniel experienced the vision, and wrote the passage, at least six hundred years before John wrote the book of Revelation. Most of the details are the same. Yet as noted, Daniel also records different details of the same experience. How could Daniel the prophet and John the apostle both witness the same event?

As with the author of Revelation, Daniel saw Jesus, the Son of Man. He added the detail that Jesus was coming with the clouds of Heaven. Daniel was watching Jesus ascending to Heaven immediately after His violent death on the cross, and His resurrection from the dead. He then recorded the very moment where the Son was reunited with the Father once again.

Note in Daniel's description, the Father is identified as the Ancient of Days. Earlier in chapter 7 this great Ancient of Days is pictured presiding over Heaven's Court. And before this throne, Jesus, resurrected, is presented before Him.

Presented! That's an unusual choice of words, isn't it? But what Daniel is seeing is more than just a family reunion between Father and Son. The word *presented* has legal applications vital to our understanding. Because it was then that Jesus presented His own body and blood as legal evidence for the redemption of mankind.

Jesus spoke of this to His disciples on the night He was betrayed. He consecrated bread, saying, *"Take, eat; this is My body"* (Matthew 26:26). Then He held up the Passover cup and declared, *"Drink from it, all of you; for this is My blood of the covenant"* (verses 27-28). His own body and blood were being presented for our redemption! According to the prophet Isaiah: *"He was wounded for our transgressions, bruised for our iniquities, the chastisement that brought us peace was laid upon Him, and with His stripes we are healed... By His knowledge the Righteous One will justify many, for He will bear their iniquities"* (Isa. 53:5, 11).

Jesus not only took on our sins; He became sin for us. The choice of Jesus to *become sin* was costly beyond our understanding. *"God's eyes are purer than to behold evil"* (Hab. 1:13). There was actually a moment in time where the boundless, eternal relationship between Jesus and His Father was severed. Where the Ancient of Days was forced to turn His face from His only begotten Son. The withdrawal was experienced at its fullest as Jesus suffered on the cross for you and me. *"My God, My God, why have you forsaken Me?"* (Matt. 27:46).

And before the heavenly reunion between Father and Son could be fully realized, a formality of unimaginable ramifications had to take place. Scriptures say that a spotless lamb alone could atone for sin. Jesus' body and blood—His very life—had to be scrutinized according to the standard of purity demanded by Heaven's Court.

Thank God the gavel has fallen for our redemption. Judgment has been rendered in favor of the saints. For all eternity!

And to Jesus was given all dominion. The scroll of mankind's redemption could finally be unsealed. By this verdict Jesus' covenant of redemption was forever established. Again, every other judgment or decree, every scroll, issues from this one verdict. It is the Precedent of all precedents.

> *"Worthy are You to take the scroll and to break its seals; for You were slaughtered, and You purchased people for God with Your blood from every tribe, language, people, and nation. You have made them to be kings and priests to our God, and they will reign upon the earth!"* (Revelation 5:9-10).

> *"Sing, barren woman.... You will forget the shame of your youth and remember no more the reproach of your widow-hood. For your Maker is your husband—the Lord Almighty is his name—the Holy One of Israel is your Redeemer; ... I hid*

my face from you for a moment, but with everlasting kindness
I will have compassion on you," says the Lord your Redeemer.
"To me this is like the days of Noah, when I swore that the
waters of Noah would never again cover the earth. So now
I have sworn not to be angry with you, never to rebuke you
again. my unfailing love for you will not be shaken nor my
covenant of peace be removed" (Isaiah 54:1, 4-5, 8-9 NIV).

The Turnaround Verdict

Again, the key to the power of the Turnaround Verdict rests within its origination. It's not a byproduct of man's discernment, logic, or will. Instead, the words recorded by Daniel convey a decision by the Court of Heaven, presided over by One who identifies Himself as the Judge of the entire earth.

Ponder the implications. That such a court even exists, let alone that its judgments can affect the thrones of earth, is staggering. In reality all nations, governments, and people have already been greatly impacted and will soon be impacted again.

Daniel 7 provides the clearest chapter in the Bible on the Court of Heaven. Throughout this visionary encounter, the prophet Daniel serves as sort of a court reporter, documenting the greatest cases in all recorded history.

Consider this, for instance. The Turnaround Verdict, recorded in Daniel 7:22, is so extraordinary in magnitude that it actually catalyzes the Great Return of Jesus Christ—followed by the promised earthly reign of this Messiah from His Covenant Land of Israel.

Let's take a brief glimpse into Daniel's vision of the Turnaround Verdict, beginning with verses 21-22: *"I kept watching, and that horn was waging war with the saints and overpowering them. Until the Ancient of Days came, and judgment was rendered in favor of the saints of the Highest One, and the time arrived when the saints took possession of the kingdom."*

Until this verdict was released, the Bible says that the saints of God were being overpowered by a demonic horn, a symbol of an antichrist spirit. Theologians have long debated whether this antichrist horn represents a spiritual entity or a human being. I personally don't know. This antichrist horn is perhaps symbolic of a human being who, like Pharaoh of old, is empowered in life and governance by a high-level demonic power. United together in covenant for evil.

The Bible implies that, at the time of this decision, the saints were doing everything they knew to do—worshiping, fasting, praying, tithing, assembling together, living righteous lives in their professions and at home. They were mobilizing to affect the seven mountains of society for God.

Yet instead of victory, they were losing ground at every turn! Isolated, divided, marginalized, impoverished, defrauded of covenant promises. Many even making the ultimate sacrifice, the flame of their very lives extinguished for their faith.

Sounds familiar, doesn't it? Way too familiar.

That's when the Court of Heaven intervenes and rules in their favor. The east that opposed them is immediately restrained. And in every dimension of life and the spirit where the saints were opposed, they suddenly win! These same war-weary believers are immediately released to possess the Kingdom.

Please note that a verdict in Heaven's Courtroom accomplishes for the saints what their own spiritual warfare and cultural engagement could not alone attain. I am by no means saying we should not engage in these things. They are vital. But they alone cannot accomplish the full purpose for which you and I invest our lives, apart from intervention by Heaven's Court.

Remember that the Lord Himself honors, upholds, and defends every verdict that He legitimately renders.

Turnaround.

Again, for the saints, it's simply a matter of time.

The National Release of Daniel 7:22

I bet you didn't know this. But the Declaration of Independence, signed on July 4, 1776, actually contains an appeal to Heaven's Court.

"We hold these truths to be self-evident, that all men are created equal, that they are endowed by their Creator with certain unalienable rights, that among these are life, liberty and the pursuit of happiness... That to secure these rights, governments are instituted among men, deriving their just powers from the consent of the governed... We, therefore, the Representatives of the United States of America, APPEALING TO THE SUPREME JUDGE OF THE WORLD for the rectitude of our intentions."

The Declaration of Independence was essentially a divorce decree from Great Britain. Within its contents is a clear list of grievances, followed by a simple plea. In their wisdom the founders invoked the Court of Heaven to judge in favor of their cause.

Evidently the verdict was granted, because literal turnarounds followed. Miracle after miracle guided the Continental Army to gain victory in the revolution against the strongest military in the known world. And the United States of America came to birth as a freedom nation.

It is interesting how God remembers. For when He desired to release the Daniel 7:22 Turnaround Verdict again to our nation, He summoned us to an historic gathering place in Boston where the American

Revolution was first mobilized. The date chosen was July 22, or 7-22, 2014.

Dutch Sheets and Chuck Pierce joined us, along with Gary Beaton, Jamie Fitt, and a host of worshipers, leaders, and intercessors from across the land.

Faneuil Hall is known as the "Womb of the Revolution" because the auditorium was a regular gathering place for our revolutionary forefathers to present their initial appeals for freedom. Revere, Adams, and Hancock were among the fiery orators. Raucous debates there compelled a small band of Bostonian tradesmen, dockworkers, rulers, and writers to make a courageous stand for freedom.

Even pastors turned revolutionaries—and soon shaped the course of history.

What stunned me is that in Hebrew, "Faneuil" or "Phanuel" literally means "the face of God." Our revolutionary forefathers were summoned before the face of God to birth the next phase of the freedom movement launched by covenant with Him.

And amazingly, we were summoned to secure a "turnaround verdict" that perpetuates His covenant in our time.

In the afternoon of 7-22, we presented our petition for the preservation of America's freedom. From the very beginning the atmosphere at this historic "Womb of Revolution" was charged with a divine presence. Hundreds showed up. Myriads more, if you count those who had gathered beyond the veil in what the Bible calls the "Great Cloud of Witnesses."

All of our leaders were very aware of the presence of these witnesses as we made our "Appeal to Heaven." It was literally as though they were standing together with us in Heaven's Court. We "knew" we were pleading their cause even more than our own. And as we together made our appeal, the sense was palpable, tangible that American history was somehow being redefined before our very eyes.

Just as Elijah waited for fire to confirm God's verdict for his land, we were compelled by the Spirit to wait for a tangible sign that He had ruled in our favor, and His gavel had come down.

The next day, we journeyed from the "Womb of the Revolution" to the "Turning Point of the Revolution" in Trenton, New Jersey, on 7-23. Turns out the meeting, hosted by apostolic leaders John and Sheryl Price, was being held in the very location where George Washington crossed the Delaware River—*and turned the tide of the American Revolution.*

From the womb of the Revolution to its turning point. Turnaround!

And that's when fire fell from Heaven. In the Trenton area, a bolt of lightning actually struck the historic estate of a signer of the Declaration of Independence named Richard Stockton. According to reports, the lightning ignited the tip of an evergreen tree, setting it on fire. But the trunk acted as a conduit, propelling this pulsating energy all the way to its roots.

Deep underground, the lightning shot from the root system of the now-smoldering evergreen into an interconnected root system of another tree—and set it on fire as well.

You know what I'm about to say. You really cannot make this stuff up.

First Priority—Turning Hearts

In a moment we're going to give you the inside story on what we perceive to be some of the most extraordinary governmental turnarounds in recent history. Because they came in conjunction with the release of this Turnaround Verdict. But as shared in chapter 1, before the Lord focused us on national turnaround, He first called us to turnarounds on the home front, within our own families. Turnaround Tuesday!

This remains our most important priority. And according to Scripture, it's actually these turnarounds which break the curse off the land nationally.

> *"Behold, I will send you Elijah the prophet before the coming of the great and dreadful day of the Lord. And he will TURN the hearts of the fathers to the children, and the hearts of the children to their fathers, lest I come and strike the earth with a curse"* (Mal. 4:5-6 NKJV).

Jerusalem—Dramatic Election Turnaround

Eight months after the Turnaround Verdict's release, Jolene and I found ourselves facing the proverbial wall. The Western Wall actually.

We were standing for God to move according to this verdict at this ancient structure in Jerusalem. With its limestone ashlars lining the western base of the Temple Mount, the Western Wall is considered the holiest site in Judaism, and is saturated with 24-7 prayer. As you already know, God considers this geographic area the center of His earthly throne.

It's really there that we gained perspective on the true scope of this Daniel 7:22 Turnaround Verdict.

We had just become witnesses to history as Israeli Prime Minister Benjamin Netanyahu won a hard-fought election. To Jolene and me this was much more than a victory in politics—*it was actually a verdict from God's throne.* An initial fulfillment of a global prayer assignment conveying how God was rendering judgment in favor of the saints, granting unprecedented turnarounds in our lives and world.

And it was a turnaround. Nobody thought Netanyahu was going to win. Especially because so much pressure had been applied by the US government against him. Netanyahu had stood alone against the Iranian nuclear accords on behalf of his land, and on behalf of the Sunni nations of the Mideast who were equally threatened by the Persian empire securing an atomic bomb. Extraordinary steps were then taken to ensure Netanyahu's downfall.

As God often does, He allowed the odds of success to dramatically decrease before bringing the impossible into reality. That's why a book on turnarounds is actually so practical. It's generally how He rolls!

Ten days before, Jolene and I were sent by the Lord to Israel to present the Daniel 7:22 Turnaround Verdict as a prophetic mandate over the election. Earlier we stood for the 2014 American elections to shift according to this verdict. In 2015, we felt strongly that the Lord was granting this same verdict and turnaround for Israel. In both cases, the results proved successful beyond anything we imagined.

> As God often does, He allowed the odds of success to dramatically decrease before bringing the impossible into reality.

And as I prayed facing this ancient wall, the word of the Lord came suddenly to me: *As you stood with Me for My elections in My Covenant Land, so I will stand with you for a turnaround in your 2016 presidential elections!*

Interestingly, the US election results of 2016 mirrored Israel's election results in 2015. God came through just as He had promised, with two of the most substantive election turnarounds in recent history. And as we mentioned in chapter 2, the turnarounds witnessed almost daily over the ensuing years were simply staggering. Many were recorded in our book *White House Watchmen.*

From my perspective, Donald Trump and Benjamin Netanyahu were both chosen by God as catalysts of His turnaround for their time. It is therefore very interesting that they both lost elections in 2020, and departed within months of each other. To address this, let me share what the Lord showed me shortly after Trump became president. He spoke to my heart: *The same verdict which brought them both into office will keep them in office as long as I desire.*

Reflecting on this word has brought great peace to my heart. Ultimately the Lord stewards the execution of His verdict His way, for His glory and the ultimate advancement of His Kingdom. And He is always initiating a new way forward!

The Second Release of Daniel 7:22

Talk about a turnaround. It seemed as though we had just been there. But after launching the Glory Train movement in Alaska over Passover, we were literally compelled by God's Spirit to return just three months later to mark the 70th anniversary of the national release of this Daniel 7:22 turnaround movement.

Remember, Chuck Pierce had prophesied that Alaska is a gateway for the Ancient of Days. Just as the first national release of the Daniel 7:22 Turnaround Verdict gave definition to a seven-year season of turnaround, I knew the Lord was summoning us to Alaska to receive a second national release. As with the Faneuil Hall verdict, I knew it would in time define the future.

The Lord confirmed this direction through yet another astounding prophecy by Chuck Pierce. Almost two years beforehand, on August 8, 2019 Chuck Pierce prophesied a two-year window to see a "breakthrough highway of glory" form from Alaska to San Diego. According to the word, this breakthrough highway would shift or turn the West Coast, and ultimately the nation. We had already planned a West Coast tour. But the moment I saw the word, I knew it literally defined our mission. Further, I knew the tour had to run between 7-22 and 8-8, securing the window Chuck prophesied. We called it the "Ancient of Days Tour."

"America Now Stands in Contempt of Heaven's Court"

Before launching the tour, we allotted some extra days for prayer in the Alaskan wilderness. Very simply, Chris Mitchell, Jolene, and I all felt it was important to seek the Lord as the Ancient of Days before launching this Ancient of Days tour.

We began to ask Him specifically for a throne room scroll defining His turnaround decree for this season. From our Passover experience with the Lord I already knew it would incorporate the Isaiah 54 turnaround.

That said, what the Lord began to reveal simply stopped me in my tracks.

"Upon review it has been determined that the government of the United States of America, weighing the totality of her actions, stands in contempt of her founding documents, including the United States Constitution. In truth, the leaders have adopted many of the very practices cited as grievances by their founders to justify the American Revolution... Therefore as with Egypt just prior to the Exodus, as with Israel just before her many descents from greatness, and as with the United States of America just before the Civil War, the government of the United States of America is hereby notified it now stands in contempt of Heaven's Court. With this warning comes a window of opportunity granted by the Ancient of Days for teshuvah or repentance."

Honestly, the words were hard to write. But by and large the rest of the decree, shared in full at the end of the chapter, is genuinely good news.

Turnaround—Your Redemption

If you remember one thing from this chapter, if only one sentence is allowed to become etched upon your heart and mind, let it be this: *Jesus loves you. He died and rose again to give you a better verdict.*

Please note that you cannot escape your past. But by His verdict you can actually repair it. You can repair your past to redeem your present, and restore God's dream for your future. Let's go there now!

Turnaround Decree 7: Turnaround Verdict—The Alaska Decree

7-22-2021, Palmer, Alaska

On the seventh anniversary of the Turnaround Verdict—Reconstitution of the United States, Faneuil Hall Boston

After much prayer, this document presents what our team believes to be a clear representation of the Daniel 7:22 Turnaround Verdict issued by the Ancient of Days for this season. It is comprised of two sections—a redemptive warning addressing the government of the United States; and a series of decrees defining God's covenant, and covenantal deliverance for the nation according to Isaiah 54, toward personal, collective, and national recovery.

"We hold these truths to be self-evident, that all men are created equal, that they are endowed by their Creator with certain unalienable rights, that among these are life, liberty and the pursuit of happiness... That to secure these rights, governments are instituted among men, deriving their just powers from the consent of the governed... We, therefore, the Representatives of the United States of America, appealing to the Supreme Judge of the world for the rectitude of our intentions" (Declaration of Independence, July 4, 1776).

INASMUCH AS THE FOUNDING DOCUMENTS OF THE UNITED STATES have secured freedom for the citizens of the United States, including governance by the consent of the governed, as endowed by their Creator; and inasmuch as the Nation was founded by covenant with the Lord Jesus Christ; and inasmuch as the Nation's founders have through the ages invoked the oversight and intervention of the Ancient of Days, the Supreme Judge of the World, for the rectitude of their intentions; and inasmuch as the citizens' Appeal to Heaven has become a ceaseless cry before the Court of Heaven in this hour; therefore it is decided that an uncommon warning for the United States of America must hereby be issued.

Upon review it has been determined that the government of the United States of America, weighing the totality of her actions, stands in contempt of her founding documents, including the United States Constitution. In truth, the leaders have adopted many of the very practices cited as grievances by their founders to justify the American Revolution. These include, but are not limited to:

1. Rulership by self-appointed elitists, often tied to idolatry, many of whom secure their seats through injustice.

2. Stewardship of seats of authority, with corresponding privileges and influences, for private or partisan gain at the expense of the nation and her citizens, defrauding them of their covenantal inheritance.

3. The willful merchandising of the sacred heritage, intellectual property and vast commodities of the nation for personal

or partisan gain, even to the extent that the security of the Nation has been severely compromised.

4. The deliberate manufacture and exacerbation of division between the citizens of the nation to secure personal or partisan gain.

5. The dictatorial imposition of elitist "moral codes" that directly counter the heart of God and clear biblical morality intended to elevate the dignity of both the individual and the nation.

6. The utilization of covert deception to control the masses and hide blatant injustice with little accountability or punitive discipline. Lawlessness within government defrauds her citizens. Truth and justice empower freedom.

7. The deliberate, gradual rescinding of personal freedoms, including religious freedom, defrauding citizens of the very unalienable rights decreed by the Declaration of Independence and secured by the US Constitution.

8. The continued weaponization of government institutions in order to threaten, leverage, marginalize or destroy for partisan or personal gain.

Therefore as with Egypt just prior to the Exodus, as with Israel just before her many descents from greatness, and as with the United States of America just before the Civil War, the government of the United States of America is hereby notified it now stands in contempt of Heaven's Court.

With this warning comes a window of opportunity granted by the Ancient of Days for *teshuvah*, defined in Hebrew as "repentance" and "turnaround that leads to recovery." As of 7-22-2021 this turnaround window opens. The full capabilities under the jurisdiction of this Court are being made available to assist. To the extent this window is accessed, the nation will remain blessed.

Turnaround Verdict—the Alaska Decree

"I kept watching, and that horn was waging war with the saints and prevailing against them, until the Ancient of Days came and judgment was rendered in favor of the saints of the Highest One, and the time arrived when the saints took possession of the kingdom" (Daniel 7:21-22—The Turnaround Verdict).

From Alaska, the 49th state, the pioneer state described as a gateway of the Ancient of Days, a decree issues that the window of opportunity is hereby preserved to complete the turnaround required to secure the continued blessing of the Nation, and retention of the sovereignty of the Nation, under God.

Breakthrough has been decreed. Alaska takes the lead. As of 7-22-21 the opening of a highway of glory from Alaska through Washington State, Oregon, and California begins a new process of shifting the west coast and the Nation into a new covenantal alignment with the Lord. This grace shall remain continually accessible through diligent stewardship and unceasing prayer.

1. Covenant of the Bride in America with God, and covenant of the Nation with God, divorced from historic idolatry, is hereby upheld and retained by Heaven's Court. Isaiah 54 clarifies the blessing concurrent with this decision (see "Contract with the Bride," chapter 4).

2. The Sovereignty of the Nation is hereby upheld and retained, restraining a Babylonian structure of dictatorship seeking to usurp the Constitutional governance of the United States of America (see Isa. 46:1).

3. The Freedom of the citizens of the Nation, as defined within the US Constitution, is hereby upheld and retained. Let it be

noted that the invitation to the state of Georgia remains to become the "Re-Constitution State" which upholds, protects, and defends the US Constitution amid a period of challenge.

4. Usurpers of godly governance shall be exposed and replaced by leaders empowering Godly governance in service to her citizens (see Isa. 22).

5. Awakening and revival, sparked by the restoration of the glory of God, has been decreed, including a restoration of holy conviction leading to *teshuvah* or repentance and turn-around (see Isa. 6; Acts 3:19).

6. The right to perceive, understand and redeem the times, both strategic windows of opportunity and chronological time, is hereby granted. Full circle, double portion! (see Eph. 5:16).

7. Decree of Reclamation granted—the covenantal right to possess, protect, and defend inheritance as defined by the Court is upheld and retained on behalf of the inheritors of the land and heritage (see Naboth's Vineyard, 1 Kings 21).

8. Rescue, turnaround, and empowerment for the sons and daughters of the land. From the 49th State to the nation, Isaiah 49:25 is hereby issued and decreed: *"Even the captives of the mighty man will be taken away, and the prey of a tyrant will be rescued; for I will contend with the one who contends with you, and I will save your children."*

THE SUPREME JUDGE

Verdicts cited in this Decree include: The Divorce Decree from Baal, Writ of Assistance, Declaration of Covenant, Reconstitution of the United States, Life Decree, the Liberty Charter, and others known but to God.

SEVEN ON A SCROLL:
Principles of Heaven's Court

The throne of God's beauty is also the Court of His justice. And how you "approach the bench" in the courts of earth is a shadow of how to receive His verdict from Heaven's Court. Here are seven principles:

1. *You Are a Lawyer.* The word *intercessor* is actually another word for "lawyer." You are invited to organize your case and present it before His throne. Through the precious blood of Jesus, your vindication has already been secured!

2. *Prayers and Petitions.* The apostle Paul wrote that we should *"pray in the Spirit with all manner of prayers and petitions"* (Eph. 6:18). A plea before the Court is also called a *petition.* One definition is "a formal written request to a court requesting judicial action on a certain matter." A petition in prayer is a legal presentation before the Judge, requesting a verdict from Heaven's Court.

3. *You are called to interact with the Court of Heaven.* As an intercessor, purchased by the blood of Jesus Christ, you are invited to stand among the "myriads" of men, women and angels standing before the throne, seeking God's justice. Learn to interact with Heaven's Court!

4. *Your Judge is the Ancient of Days.* Father God is specifically presented as the Ancient of Days in reference to the court. As the Ancient of Days, God sees all days and can render judgment to deliver you from the encroachment of generational bondages.

5 *The Lord will review your case.* When the court sits, the books, or scrolls, are opened. God will review your petition in light of the past, present, and future. More on this in the next chapter!

6. *You can see principalities disengaged from your life.* Daniel saw the greatest evil forces disengaged from humanity by a throne room verdict. So did Joshua, as pictured in Zechariah 3. Through the justification of the body and blood of Jesus Christ, you can too—in your own life, family, and your world.

7. *Ask God to rule in favor of the saints!* So many times we petition the court without ever asking for a verdict. Then we wonder why nothing has changed. King David was an expert at this. He was specific, and he always asked God to rule in his favor. Lawyers don't just ask for favorable verdicts; they define them for their judge. Seek God's face. And ask Him to render verdict in your favor!

CHAPTER 8

BACK TO THE FUTURE

"Wait a minute, Doc. Are you telling me you built a time machine... out of a DeLorean?" —Michael J. Fox, *Back to the Future*

AS OUR BOOK HAS CHRONICLED, many challenges have befallen our nation. But hang in there, forerunner. They can turn in a moment! You can learn to repair the past to redeem the present and secure God's dream for the future. And as you will see, perceiving and declaring God's decrees is a primary catalyst for this process. It's like a flux capacitor in the Spirit!

In case you're not up on 1980s time-travel technology, *flux* is another word for "flow." *Capacitor* is a word that describes the storage of power, specifically electricity. So a flux capacitor releases the power for you to flow through the epochs, eras, and ages that constitute time. In essence, to travel—*Back to the Future.*

It was through a very long flight from Alaska to Seattle that my attention became drawn to this Hollywood classic. Just a day before, on 7-22-2021, our team launched the Ancient of Days tour and decreed and open window to complete God's intended turnaround. Searching for movies to occupy my time, *Back to the Future* seemed like the cleanest of the selections. And it was a bit nostalgic. I actually graduated high school the year it was released.

You probably know the plot already. A young Michael J. Fox is propelled 30 years back in time by souped-up DeLorean, invented by his mad-scientist mentor, Doc. Included in the amenities of this fine luxury automobile is a new invention which enables time travel. A flux capacitor! Again, the capacitor part provides energy that propels the DeLorean backward or forward through the flux, or flow, of time.

Which is good news. Because it turned out that 1955 wasn't all it's cracked up to be. So Marty and Doc must literally repair the past to redeem their present world—1985—and restore the future to its original intention.

Crazy. And the farther into this crazy movie I got, the more I realized something even more astounding. God was actually using the movie to speak to me. Even to confirm some profound spiritual explorations at a very deep level. For instance: "I've calculated the distance and wind resistance retroactive from the moment the lightning strikes, AT EXACTLY 7 MINUTES and 22 SECONDS. When this alarm goes off, you hit the gas!"

Yes, it's true. Exactly 7 minutes and 22 seconds is the timing featured for the breakthrough by a mad scientist hanging from a clock tower, where a lightning bolt is conveniently predestined to strike. The surge of energy from the bolt becomes fuel for the flux capacitor. A time gate then opens, and Marty gets propelled—BACK TO THE FUTURE!

Crazy. Given God's emphasis on Daniel 7:22 especially, you can't make this stuff up.

And then there's this.

The DeLorean needed to attain a speed of exactly 88 miles an hour to harness the power of this lightning strike. Only when the speedometer hit 88 mph could the "time gate" be accessed. In an unimaginable way this detail spoke to us too, seeing how the Ancient of Days Tour was marked by God from 7-22 in Alaska to 8-8 in San Diego, California.

We had chosen 8-8 to close out the tour because this was the date highlighted when Chuck Pierce prophesied about a two-year window for a "breakthrough highway of glory" to form from Alaska through all of California.

Oh, did I mention that California was the location where the movie *Back to the Future* was set? Not far from we were headed on 8-8.

Michael J. Fox returns home from 1955 to 1985, only to find that his family life has drastically improved. Mom is beautiful. Dad is a conqueror instead of a victim. The past has been repaired, the present world redeemed, and times ahead look bright! All made possible by a time machine that enabled him to, well, repair the past.

GREAT SCOTT! Would you believe a bolt of lightning struck the Washington Monument—literally moments after we touched down in Washington, DC, returning from the

> "I've calculated the distance and wind resistance retroactive from the moment the lightning strikes, AT EXACTLY 7 MINUTES and 22 SECONDS. When this alarm goes off, you hit the gas!"

Ancient of Days Tour! Because of the sudden lightning storm, our plane remained on the tarmac of Reagan National for almost an hour.

I don't know the gigawatts. But the jolt of lightning that hit the Washington Monument was actually so strong it had to be shut down completely for four entire days. All the circuits were blown, essentially "unplugging" the Washington Monument from its power source! Kind of like that clock tower in the movie...

You know what I'm about to say. Can't make this stuff up!

Just in case you were wondering—Jolene and I took it as a sign. From coast to coast, judgment has been rendered in favor of the saints. Our

Jon Hamill looks over the "Back to the Future" DeLorean by the US Capitol on the National Mall. Photo: Jolene Hamill

national covenant with God had been secured. The Daniel 7:22 Turnaround Verdict has been reissued for our nation. In an uncanny way this verdict was confirmed once again by fire from Heaven, just as the original release of Daniel 7:22 was confirmed by a lightning strike seven years beforehand.

And a turnaround window has opened once again.

But wait, there's actually more! Just days before the twentieth anniversary of September 11, the same DeLorean used in the movie actually descended on the National Mall—right between the Washington Monument and the US Capitol! It came complete with a flux capacitor, a time machine dashboard with a digital speedometer, and a California license plate that said "Outta Time."

All proof it's now time to go BACK TO THE FUTURE.

"Tell me, Future Boy, who's President of the United States in 1985?" Doc exclaims.

"Ronald Reagan," Marty replies.

Doc laughs. "Ronald Reagan? The actor? Ha! Then who's Vice President, Jerry Lewis?"

A Few Takeaways

Back to the Future...

Is this a word from the Lord? If so, what does the mandate mean? Let's start with the simplest shift first. Jolene saw how God is calling us to shift from focusing predominantly on the past to dreaming with Him about a better future. In other words, He is calling us to shift our focus from present-past to present-future. This simple transition is so much more important than words can convey.

> Lord is once more releasing a Daniel 7:22 turnaround movement. He is opening a profound window to repair the past and redeem the present to secure His intentions for the future.

Second, on a broader level, the Lord is once more releasing a Daniel 7:22 turnaround movement. In a way Marty and Doc can only watch in envy, He is opening a profound window to repair the past and redeem the present to secure His intentions for the future.

Another facet worth exploring is actually the endless capacities that lie within...your mouth. Your mouth, declaring God's decree, is like a flux capacitor, with the inherent capacity to affect the past, the present and the future. You shall decree a thing, and it shall be established!

And what really propels your mouth across the thresholds is a capacitor. It's like a lightning strike—a surge of Holy Spirit power!

Note that lightning, or fire from Heaven, can be seen as a symbol confirming both covenant and covenant restoration. After King David repented for his sins, fire came from Heaven to light up the altar he had built. Then fire came down from Heaven when Solomon consecrated the Temple to the Lord. Elijah rebuilt an altar of covenant which the prophets of Baal had cast down. Heaven's fire that day confirmed to all Israel that the Lord was indeed God, and that He had restored their hearts back to Him.

And now a fourth takeaway: Every budding trailblazer needs a mad scientist time traveler to mentor them along life's epic journey. In our world we like to call them prophets.

Redeeming the Time

Did you know that many prophets have received encounters with the Lord over time? Not only that, but a primary responsibility of prophets is to gain understanding of the times, and even to repair breaches that have occurred through time.

"This is the vision I had," recounted the late Bob Jones, one such visionary prophet. He saw a "Glory Train," representing a new move of God where His glory is being restored to cities, regions, and nations.

In Bob's experience the Conductor took his ticket. "Then He gave me an egg," Bob continued. "And I said, 'What is this egg? What's inside this egg?' The Conductor said, 'Time! You see, there was no time before man. Time was created for man. And in this egg there is yesterday's, today's, and tomorrow's time. And every time you hear the train whistle it will remind you of the coming glory!'"[1]

An egg is a time capsule. Try to wrap your head around that one. But the Conductor's revelation is profoundly biblical. God lives outside of time. He releases His eternal revelation and decrees into the seconds, minutes, hours, days, years, and eras we know as chronological time, or *chronos* time in Greek. He also creates "time gates" or windows of opportunity, defined in Greek as *kairos* time.

He also compels us to access His power to redeem time. This is actually an apostolic mandate for both kairos times and chronos times.

"See then that you walk circumspectly, not as fools but as wise, redeeming the time, because the days are evil" (Eph. 5:15-16).

The question, of course, is how?

Chuck Pierce asked it this way: "Is there a Creator who transcends and enters time to commune with His children so they may efficiently walk in time? When you mess up in one season, can He make you capable of redeeming the times or buying back wasted time?"[2]

The good news is, of course, YES. You can partner with the Lord to redeem your kairos and even chronos times. Note that the prophet Daniel had no time-travel technology to accomplish his mission. But he was called to heal the history of his people—literally to repair the past to

Note that the prophet Daniel had no time-travel technology to accomplish his mission. But he was called to heal the history of his people—literally to repair the past to redeem the present, and restore God's dream for the future.

187

redeem the present, and restore God's dream for the future. That's your calling as well.

And as you will see, many of God's decrees actually carry with them an inherent power to redeem the time.

God as the Ancient of Days

It has been said that the seraphim, who stand night and day before God's eternal throne, fall prostrate so often because they are continually overwhelmed by experiencing new facets of His glory. The awe of His majesty. The poignancy of His justice. The breathtaking beauty of His countenance. From the center of the throne these revelations crash like waves upon His creation, and those closest in proximity become the first to experience them.

Bottom line—every fresh move of the Spirit carries with it a fresh revelation of God. And as part of this turnaround movement, Holy Spirit is highlighting a revelation of God as the Ancient of Days.

There is only one chapter in the entirety of the Bible where God is conveyed by the name "Ancient of Days." That is in Daniel 7:9-10: *"I kept looking until thrones were set up, and the Ancient of Days took His seat... Thousands upon thousands were serving Him, and myriads upon myriads were standing before Him; the court convened, and the books were opened."*

Daniel sees the Lord in His majesty taking His seat at the throne. Why is He conveyed here as the Ancient of Days? His "ancient-ness" alone does not qualify Him to rule. For instance Satan is an eternal being is well. He is eternally given to evil. Further, the days of mankind neither increase or decrease His internal capacities. God is qualified to rule because His unlimited integrity, His boundless competence, His inherent goodness, and His absolute power never dissipate over time. He is the same, yesterday, today, and forever.

Further, the Lord is identified as the Ancient of Days because He presides over the past, the present, and the future. God is the Creator of time, but He exists outside of time. It is for this reason that you can partner with Him to repair the past, redeem your present, and secure His dream for your future.

Much like the apostle John in Revelation, the prophet Daniel sees myriads and myriads of angelic hosts and redeemed human beings worshiping Him and attending to their respective duties. After the Ancient of Days takes His seat, the Court is then seated, and the scrolls are opened. Court is in session!

It's so important to understand this scene conveys an eternal reality that is still going on today. The throne of God's matchless beauty is also the Court of His justice. Right now, wherever you are, you and I can join the myriads of angelic hosts and redeemed human beings now worshiping before His throne. You can also present your case and receive a verdict in your favor!

Daniel in this experience functioned much like a courtroom scribe. As such he recorded the most important verdicts granted to humanity through the ages. As already noted, the prophet saw Jesus presented, His body and blood given for the redemption of mankind. He then saw dominion transferred to the Son of Man, just as the apostle John saw the scrolls transferred from the Father's hand. Further, Daniel saw the Turnaround Verdict in all its capacities rendered in favor of the saints.

Repairing the Scroll of Your Generational Line

So let's go back to the future for a moment. As the Ancient of Days, the Lord knows firsthand all of the sins your forefathers committed, as well as their consequences then and through your generational line. Sexual immorality, covenant breaking, unjust bloodshed, theft and perjury, abuse—the list goes on. He also saw the positive decisions your forefathers made, releasing generational blessings. All were carefully recorded as part of Heaven's legal records for each and every life (see Dan. 7:10).

Heaven documents our actions in this life, evil and good, as well as their ramifications over our entire generational line. In our age of instant information, vast computer storage, and NSA monitoring, this idea does not sound so far-fetched. But the administrative capacities alone to accomplish this magnitude of record keeping probably provoked the ancients to either disbelief or extreme fear. Maybe some of you reading this are now terrified, especially if you are not right with the Lord. Because the consequences of your decisions in this life are eternal. And the wages of sin remains death.

But let's get to the "repairing" part of this message. It's really cool. We know that Jesus alone has redeemed us from our sin through His body and blood. As a steward of this covenant, you can actually ask the Ancient of Days to open the scrolls of your generational line and review its contents. Like Daniel, you can confess your sins and the iniquities of your fathers before His throne. You can ask Him to blot out these sins and iniquities through the body and blood of Jesus Christ!

You obviously don't know about every blockage or reproach in your generational line. But as the Ancient of Days, He does. Recorded in these scrolls is the time Grandpa made pacts with demonic idols to gain something he didn't feel God would grant. Also recorded is the legal claim by these powers that has held your generational line in captivity from that time forward.

And the good news is that you can ask God to open the books, review your case, and annul every legal covenant or pact with hell that your forefathers made—that now claims your generational line (see Isa. 28). Before Heaven's Court, you can commit your bloodline to Him and ask Him to cleanse, restore, and redeem!

What's more, you today have even more of a legal precedent to receive forgiveness—for your sins and the sins of your forefathers—than even Daniel.

> *"I, I alone, am the one who wipes out your wrongdoings for My own sake, and I will not remember your sins. Meet Me in court, let's argue our case together"* (Isa. 43:25-6).

You might be wondering what deliverance from generational bondages has to do with releasing turnaround decrees. Granted, we are not teaching you here about the intricacies on receiving and releasing them. Instead we are teaching you how to remove the reproaches, even in your generational line, that may hinder your turnaround decree from coming to pass.

This brings up a great point. As we've covered, some scrolls are meant by God to be decreed and released. Yet some are meant to be erased. God wants to remove these reproaches from your present record, and the record of your generational line. It's time for you to approach the bench!

Speaking of which...

Zechariah 3—the Original "Back to the Future"

With the help of his mad scientist prophetic father, the word *turnaround* took on a whole new meaning for Marty McFly as he traveled back in time to repair his family's severe dysfunction. Mama bounced forward into her most stunning self. Papa grew Delta Force tendencies, becoming wildly successful after overcoming a self-deflating cowardice that had haunted him from childhood. Their romance became fire.

And best of all, Biff the bully became the family servant.

In short, Marty repaired the past to redeem the present and secure a better future for all. Including his girl, who became his loyal companion for future time-gate repair work. Securing this potential alone should make time travel an existential pursuit!

Of course, scientists have yet to bridge the vast realms and dimensions of what we know as time. So what Marty achieved on camera seems to be just very pleasant fiction.

Except that it's not. The core story is actually as old as the Bible. Which should not be too much of a surprise, seeing that the Ancient of Days is the author. Like *Back to the Future*, it even includes a mad scientist prophetic father—minus the mad scientist part. And his flux capacitor was actually the Turnaround Tuesday prayer movement of his time.

The prophetic father is named Zechariah, author of the prophetic book by his name. The Marty McFly of the Old Testament is a young protege of his named Joshua, who was serving as high priest of Israel at the time the time-repairing incident occurred.

Joshua had inherited an impossible situation. As high priest of God's Covenant Land, he had been appointed steward of His restoration movement after the prolonged disaster of Babylonian exile. While carpenters rebuilt the structure of the Temple, Joshua was responsible for rebuilding the essence of priestly ministry and Jewish community. You could say he was called to restore the worship movement of his era, connecting Heaven and earth again in Jerusalem.

Maybe it's not a coincidence that Joshua the high priest was named after both Joshua, the military leader who led his people into the Promised Land generations before, and Yeshua, the Redeemer of mankind, who, as you will see, redeemed even him.

Freedom from Generational Sin and Bondages

I'm sure Joshua longed for personal encounters with God similar to what his forefathers had experienced. But when the request was granted, it may not have been quite what he had expected. Similar to many of his predecessors, Joshua was caught up before the throne. The Lord was holding court. And Joshua essentially came before the Ancient of Days as a prisoner.

> *"Then he showed me Joshua the high priest standing before the angel of the Lord, and Satan standing at his right to accuse him. And the Lord said to Satan, 'The Lord rebuke you, Satan! Indeed, the Lord who has chosen Jerusalem rebuke you! Is this not a brand snatched from the fire?'"* (Zech. 3:1-2).

Note that Joshua was having an experience with God that his prophetic father Zechariah was watching, and perhaps had even initiated through his intercession for the young protege. Let me emphasize this. If you want to encounter God, earnestly contend in prayer for your spiritual sons and daughters, and your natural sons and daughters. Make the investment!

In Zechariah's vision the Lord sat as Judge. The angel of the Lord, most likely Jesus in His preincarnate state, served as the defense attorney. Satan stood before the Court as the prosecuting attorney. And Joshua was dragged into court as the accused. What a way to be introduced to throne room scenes! But for Joshua, the proceedings soon turned dramatically in his favor. The Lord rebuked Satan. And He began the process of restoring Joshua. A team surrounded Joshua to execute God's decrees.

Now, it's important to understand that Satan's accusations carried extreme legitimacy. In fact, the very clothes Joshua wore were bearing witness to his sin.

> *"Now Joshua was clothed in filthy garments and was standing before the angel. And he responded and said to those who were standing before him, saying, 'Remove the filthy garments from him.' Again he said to him, 'See, I have taken your iniquity away from you and will clothe you with festive robes'"* (Zech. 3:3-4).

In this courtroom scene, all Satan had to do is essentially discern the evidence of crimes embedded in the clothing Joshua was wearing. They were so obvious that you'd probably wonder how this high priest could have put so much unrighteous living into such a short time on earth.

But note God's response. Remove the filthy robe! And that action represented the removal of his iniquity. In other words, not just his present sin but the accumulated generational sin that had been weighing Joshua down.

Which explains the high content of defilement on the priestly robes. It's important to understand that the robes of a priest were passed down from generation to generation. Each ensuing generation of priests inherited a robe from their priestly forefathers. They would be commissioned with a fresh anointing, with fresh oil poured over their heads and on to these robes. By this each new generation of priests would wear a mantle that carried both the anointings from previous generations as well as a fresh anointing for their hour.

Which is profound. At least until the anointing became compromised with sin.

Then generational sins began to accumulate on these very robes. Actually the very sins which provoked God to remove them from the Promised Land into Babylonian captivity.

This makes the imagery of Joshua's iniquity being removed even more telling. The Lord delivered him from the accumulated sins of generations of priests who had compromised their integrity before the Lord. You can imagine how that robe had and confined him.

Freedom was costly though. Given the legitimacy of Satan's accusations, for God the Father to genuinely rebuke Satan and redeem Joshua there was only one way. Another Joshua, Yeshua the King and High Priest, was required to be sentenced to death in Joshua's place to atone for both his sin and the sins of his forefathers.

> *"Then I said, 'Have them put a clean headband on his head.'*
> *So they put the clean headband on his head and clothed him*
> *with garments, while the angel of the Lord was standing by"*
> (Zech. 3:5).

Suddenly a decree was interjected from someone other than the Lord Himself. Zechariah, in the Spirit while in prayer for his young protege, becomes an active participant with the angels in the young priest's deliverance! And through his decree a dimension of supernatural covering became restored.

God wants to fully restore His covering over you personally, as well as over your family and sphere. Much of this comes from the process of healing and deliverance from generational bondages. I can also say from experience there is something missing in your journey until you receive the covering of genuine mothers and fathers in the Lord.

Suddenly Joshua was granted a new lease on life. The end of his road became for him a gateway into new beginnings. Not only did he become free, from the inside out. A fresh mantle was granted to cover him again. The Lord restored His covenant covering, minus the defilement.

Watch this now. Because Joshua was then *recommissioned* into the very position he originally held. This time he was even granted unhindered access to the throne. This is the ultimate dream of every true priest of the Lord.

But in addition, this former prisoner was given charge to govern God's house, and even His courts!

> *"And the angel of the Lord admonished Joshua, saying, 'The Lord of armies says this: "If you walk in My ways and perform My service, then you will both govern My house and be in charge of My courts, and I will grant you free access among these who are standing here"'"* (Zech. 3:6-7).

Generational sin is a heavy garment that was never meant for you to carry. It weighs down your life, your friendships, your work and world. It draws rejection, accusation, and sabotage. And worst of all, it weighs down your relationship with God.

Through the same body and blood which freed you from your personal sins, you have also been redeemed from the sins of your fathers, your mothers, from your generational line. But as with salvation, this miracle investment must also be appropriated. There is often a lot of work involved in seeing His redemption fully manifested in your life, but it is worth it all. You will gain a much deeper reality of the born-again experience.

It is time for a new identity, completely separated from the past. It's time for old mantles to be removed and new mantles to be received from Heaven for the new season we are in. The mantle of the Ancient of Days!

And like Joshua, it is time for you to gain a new commissioning into both fresh intimacy with God, and higher authority to rule.

Zechariah—Model of Prophetic Fathering

As a prophetic father, Zechariah was watching after Joshua in prayer when the Lord released him into this transcendent prophetic experience. He saw Joshua's condition from a throne room perspective. And he prayed Joshua through until the weight of iniquity had been removed, and the high priest was recommissioned at a much higher level.

And that's exactly the results we aim to attain as we begin to pray over our children. It's such a key part of their development. Faith works by love. And as you pray you will see your own heart turning again to your kids. You will gain God's secrets for them. And in a *Back to the Future* kind of way, you may even see a redemption of destiny secured that bridges times and epochs.

Zechariah was first a mentor, a father to Joshua. Today's budding priesthood needs your mentoring and intercessory intervention more than we may really understand. It is exactly the same with maturing leaders in government and other spheres. Zechariah came alongside an immature, not fully delivered high priest who had been assigned the task of restoring communion between Heaven and earth. My point? If you want God to shift the nation, begin by coming alongside His imperfect sons and daughters who've been summoned to catalyze His restoration!

Also, Zechariah wasn't out on a fault-finding mission to deal with Joshua's sin. The prophet was in the Spirit in prayer for the young priest when God brought him into this encounter. Presumably it was Turn-around Tuesday. And Zechariah was contending for a spiritual son!

> Zechariah was first a mentor, a father to Joshua. Today's budding priesthood needs your mentoring and intercessory intervention more than we may really understand. It is exactly the same with maturing leaders in government and other spheres.

Zechariah 3 Model—Prayer Teams

That said, every leader needs the blessing that Joshua received. Through healing and deliverance from present and generational bondages, the weights and obstructions accumulated in the bloodline become removed. The gates of sabotage in a person's life become shut. They become free to soar with the Lord in a whole new way! And their rulership increases exponentially in effectiveness.

How is this achieved? One of the most important revelations within Zechariah 3 is a team approach to intercession for a leader. The whole team was before the throne along with Joshua, surrounding him. We have personally found that a team approach to intercession for a leader has proven extremely effective.

Consider building a team to cover your pastor or others assigned to your watch. You will gain from being made strong by what every joint supplies.

Zechariah and team were moved by the Spirit to decree–in their case what they were perceiving in real time. "By My Spirit" is the most powerful secret, and often the most missing secret, to holistic deliverance.

Second, decrees of renunciation often need to be made by the person to gain lasting breakthrough over generational sins and pacts with the enemy. The enemy gains a foothold in every generational line through pacts and decrees made through a person's free will, such as those made by initiates into freemasonry or other occult orders. Often these decrees include committing the entire generational line to the occult forces being invoked. Therefore, as an act of a person's will they must be repudiated and replaced by decrees covenant consecration to the Lord Jesus Christ.

Redeeming Your Scrolls of Destiny

Like Joshua under the weight of his sin, you may at some time have felt disqualified to attain the covenant destiny the Lord desires for you. Maybe you feel it's simply too late. It's not! Jesus is not only the Redeemer of your life, but the Redeemer of your time.

Let's return to a vision we shared in the beginning of the book. Scrolls of destiny were being rereleased by Jesus from His throne. He redeemed both the time, and the covenant destiny we were invited to attain. We mentioned the vision in brief, but in light of what we've now learned it's worth exploring more fully.[3]

As recounted in chapter 4s, back in 2019 the Lord gave me a visionary experience that has proven very key for today. In the vision I was ascending through the sea of glass before God's throne. As described in Revelation 15, it was mingled with fire.

I thrust my head above the waters and saw Jesus. He was shining in His majesty! My intuitive reaction was actually holy fear and awe, both to see and be seen. So I literally ducked back into the water. While praying into the vision, I sense the Lord is wanting us all to experience both profound cleansing and renewed vision of His holiness and majesty. The pure in heart will see God!

> Through healing and deliverance from present and generational bondages, the weights and obstructions accumulated in the bloodline become removed. The gates of sabotage in a person's life become shut.

When I looked again in the vision, I immediately found myself on the other side of a large table being used by Jesus as a desk. He had regathered a large stack of crumpled paper which had obviously been thrown away. One by one, Jesus took the crumpled balls of paper and placed them with care into the sea of glass. I kept watching as each scroll unfolded in the waters. In my vision, the first scroll Jesus placed in the waters was actually the Mayflower Compact.

Faded, smudged ink was restored to precision. The messages of these scrolls were literally being reconstituted before my eyes and then released through the sea to the earth.

Jesus baptizing scrolls? This may seem strange until you realize that He considers your life to be a scroll. And in your baptism is reconstitution!

"YOU are our letter (scroll), written in our hearts, known and read by all men; being manifested that you are a letter of Christ, cared for by us, written not with ink but with the Spirit of the living God, not on tablets of stone but on tablets of human hearts" (2 Cor. 3:2-3).

I also sensed the scrolls being reconstituted represent invitations and commissions from Jesus which had been thrown away. Some had been trashed intentionally, simply rejected by those who received them. Some had been trashed by people in authority over the ones who were supposed to receive them. Some were clearly sabotaged by the enemy. Some ended up in the trash bin simply out of neglect, unbelief, and disobedience. Some, like Jeremiah's title deed, were sown as seeds to establish God's legal precedent through the future.

And some scrolls represented portions of Scripture which were rejected because they were either offensive or beyond the revelatory paradigm of those who read them.

Whatever the case, know that the Lord is rereleasing many scrolls to the earth that had been crumpled up and rejected. Many revelations, commissions, and invitations are being rereleased as the Ancient of Days redeems the time on your behalf. Watch how many missed opportunities come full circle in this hour. Your reconstituted scroll is the TITLE DEED to many reconstituted windows of opportunity!

Again, the comprehensiveness of our salvation in Israel's Messiah is simply astonishing. In light of current circumstances, I hope this speaks deeply to you. God can redeem the time. You have been granted an inheritance. And the time has come to possess this resurrected deed. Back to the future!

Turnaround Decree 8: Annulling Generational Pacts with Darkness

By Martin Frankena and Jon & Jolene Hamill

> *"Your covenant with death will be annulled, and your agreement with Sheol will not stand"* (Isaiah 28:18).

Father God, I come before the Court of Heaven and petition You as the Ancient of Days to review my case and judge in my favor. I am asking that You annul all covenants established in the spirit and natural realms between myself and spiritual entities other than the Lord Jesus Christ.

Father God, as Daniel saw, I ask now that You convene court and review my case. Open the books of my life and generations. Please identify all places where either I or my forefathers entered into covenant with demonic powers. According to Isaiah 28:18, please annul all trilateral covenants, all covenants with Baal, death, and darkness throughout my generational line. I personally repent and renounce all personal and generational covenants, and I forgive my ancestors for entering into these covenants. I renounce all covenants made between myself and these entities, and I renounce all covenants made between my forefathers and these entities.

Father God, my justification in this request is simply the body and blood of Jesus Christ. Jesus took the full punishment for my sins and iniquities, or generational sins. By this precious blood, I ask that You now blot out the record of my covenants with Baal and other idols and demonic powers, and those of my forefathers.

Further, I ask that You dismiss Baal from my life and bloodline, as well as all forces under Baal that have been empowered by these covenants. Please dismantle all seats of authority, where demonic powers have had legal authority to rule over my generations through these covenants. Please grant me a judicial restraining order against these demonic powers, in Jesus' Name. Let this restraining order be enforced beginning now!

I now reset covenant with You, Father God, in the Name of Jesus Christ. I give myself to You without reserve—spirit, soul, and body. I give to You the seat of authority over myself, my family, my possessions, and my generational line. Father God, I am asking to be betrothed to the Lord Jesus Christ, and Christ alone, redeemed by His body and blood alone. I receive Jesus Christ as My Lord, Savior, Bridegroom, and King. In Jesus' Name, AMEN!

SEVEN ON A SCROLL:
Great Lines from "Back to the Future!"[4]

1. "Wait a minute, Doc. Are you telling me you built a time machine... out of a DeLorean?" (Marty McFly to Doc).

2. "Great Scott!" (Doc).

3. "It's your kids, Marty! Something's gotta be done about your kids!" (Doc).

4. "Nobody calls me chicken!" (Marty McFly).

5. "Roads? Where we're going, we don't need roads" (Doc).

6. "I guess you guys aren't ready for that yet. But your kids are gonna love it!" (Marty McFly).

7. "Tell me, Future Boy, who's President of the United States in 1985?" Doc asks. "Ronald Reagan," Marty replies. "Ronald Reagan? The actor? Ha! Then who's Vice President, Jerry Lewis?"

8. BONUS QUOTE: "If my calculations are correct, when this baby hits 88 miles per hour, you're gonna see some serious S(TUFF)!" (Doc).

PART 4

The FINISHING DECREE

CHAPTER 9

A Door Stands Open

"He who is holy, who is true, who has the key of David, who opens and no one will shut, and who shuts and no one opens, says this: 'I know your deeds. Behold, I have put before you an open door which no one can shut.' ... After these things I looked, and behold, a door standing open in heaven, and the first voice which I had heard, like the sound of a trumpet speaking with me, said, "Come up here, and I will show you what must take place after these things" (Revelation 3:7-8; 4:1).

RECENTLY THE LORD GAVE ME AN INTERESTING WORD for this gateway season beginning in 2022. He said simply, *I am sevening your 22s.* Remember that seven Hebraically represents covenant. At your invitation He is coming into covenant with you over the gateway years of 2022 and beyond. According to Isaiah 22:22, which says, *"Then I will put the key of the house of David on his shoulder; when he opens, no one will shut, when he shuts, no one will open,"* He is also opening for you a door that no man can shut—even to God's very throne.

Toward the end of the chapter, we are going to teach you how to enter into covenant with Him at the threshold of your gateways.

It is interesting how the Lord brought the book *Turnaround Decrees* through the gates in 2022. Prophetically we believe the book itself marks the opening of a door for the Body of Christ to receive revelation that frames the future—even concerning the end times.

This is how the Lord encountered Jolene especially at the very beginning of 2022. He showed her an open door to gain revelation that will advance us even through end-time challenges.

I consider myself to be prophetic. But it's quite an adventure to be married to a woman who so naturally lives out her prophetic calling night and day. Jolene is always leaning into the Lord, with no striving whatsoever. Day and night she's always on watch. And the Lord always meets her, especially in dreams.

Like the time when we were first married and Jolene was shown key aspects of the coming revival. Holy Spirit moved upon her in a dream. Even though she was fast asleep she began to shake under His power. She then woke up speaking the words "Bigger than Finney! Bigger than Finney!"

With big eyes and a pounding heart, she then turned to me and asked, "Who's Finney?"

I almost wept. And not out of the profoundness of the experience either. Over decades I had been in hot pursuit of a Third Great Awakening similar to what Jonathan Edwards and revivalist Charles Finney had both experienced. Fasting. Praying. Researching. Working toward a sweeping move in our time.

I labored hard. Yet Jolene's the one who received a foretaste of it! Amazingly, she didn't even know who Charles Finney was.

That's a word for all of us, by the way. What's coming from God's heart and hand in this season is bigger even than what we've seen in times past. Bigger than Finney!

A Door Stands Open

Fast-forward to 3:20 a.m. on January 4, 2022. That's when Jolene told me, "Someone's knocking at the door!"

Well, she sort of told me. She once again was asleep at the time. It turned out she was having another significant encounter, profound in its implications and activated in real time. Here's Jolene's story, in her own words:

In early January 2022 I had the most amazing experience. It was a dream but more than a dream; it was a prophetic encounter where I was hearing clearly in the spirit realm. I dreamed that I was hearing a faint knock at my front door. I was thinking in the dream that someone should go answer. The knock came a second time, and this time it was much louder. In my dream it became clear to me that I was the one who was to answer the door. Preparing to get up, I looked at the clock on my phone and saw that it was exactly 3:20 am. I knew in my spirit that I was hearing Revelation 3:20 in a very intimate experience with my Savior.

The experience was so real that I began to head for the door to answer. It took me a minute to focus, and realize that there was really no one at the door at 3:20 in the morning. At least nobody we would actually want to welcome. As in many experiences sometimes I just know things. In this experience I knew Revelation 3:20 and subsequent verses were being highlighted by the Lord. *"Behold, I stand at the door and knock,"* reverberated in the spirit. Loud and clear. I grabbed my Bible to get more understanding and see what the Lord would show me further.

Reading the verse, I was astonished. *"Behold, I stand at the door and knock; if anyone hears My voice and opens the door, I will come in to him and dine with him, and he with Me."* It was as if the Lord was literally knocking at my door!

Later in the morning I continued praying through the experience. Revelation 3:20 was cross-referenced with another key passage of Scripture: Luke 12:36-37 (NKJV). I want to start at verses 34-35 for clarification of the passage.

"For where your treasure is, there your heart will be also. Let your waist be girded and your lamps burning; and you yourselves be like men who wait for their master, when he will return from the wedding, that when he comes and knocks they may open to him immediately. Blessed are those servants whom the master, when he comes, will find watching. Assuredly, I say to you that he will gird himself and have them sit down to eat, and will come to serve them."

The experience continued, and I knew it then transitioned to Revelation 4:1.

After these things I looked, and behold, a door standing open in heaven, and the first voice which I heard, like a trumpet speaking with me, said, "Come up here, and I will show you what must take place after these things."

I have learned when I have these experiences to sit with the Lord and commune with Him over them. I want to share with you what I feel Jesus is emphasizing through this experience.

First, the time I had this dream was during the last watch of the night. This watch is the one that ends the night season and sets the atmosphere for the new day. Jon keeps saying that we're moving through the midnight hour. We are ending the night season we have all been in, and lessons learned through this dream will set up the atmosphere for our new day that is dawning.

Second, the dream is sequential in many ways. It is about having ears to hear. The knocks became louder, and the intentionality became stronger, with each progressive knock. The whole of Scripture is calling forth *"he who has ears to hear."* It was important that although I heard the first faint knock, I did not respond. I thought someone else would answer, someone who was closer to the door and could do it easier because it would have been more convenient for them.

But the knock was not for them, it was for me. It wasn't enough to hear both knocks. The Lord was looking for a response. Just like in Song of Solomon 5:4-5:6, Jesus was by the latch of the door, and although she was yearning for him, she waited too long and he was gone. His yearning is shown in his knock—louder and louder he knocks with urgency. He loves the inconvenient times; my hesitation to answer at that hour is very telling.

With that in mind, it is interesting to note the scriptural context of this experience. It is given in the midst of the rebuke to the Laodicean church—the one that is neither hot nor cold, the one who thinks they are rich and need nothing although they are naked, poor, and blind from the Lord's perspective. He counsels them to buy gold refined in the fire. The fire, the flame that so many of us are unfortunately standing afar off from. The flame that we have let dim. Not because we don't love him but more because the flame has dimmed in the waiting and in the disappointment.

Maybe you can identify. You hear the knock, in whatever way the Lord communicates it to you, but figure someone else should answer. Maybe you think to yourself, *Would someone closer, someone more qualified, please answer the door!*

Maybe for you this story itself is a knock at your door. Don't wait for someone else to respond. You open the door for Him. Answering the knock more quickly is what the Lord wants of us all. If we make the effort, the corresponding promise is that He will come and dine with us! He will draw close in a personal way to you, dine with you, commune with you.

It is interesting that the passage in Luke talks about Jesus girding himself and serving us at the dinner table. I don't so much want to be served by Him as much as I want to sit with Him, dine with Him, be loved by Him.

Unfortunately as we let the flame dim, or as we back down our desire to reduce the pain, we lose the opportunity to make it to the Revelation 4 experience. The door that stands open in Heaven, the voice that is as loud as a trumpet, the ascending before the throne to see. It's in this place where the voice is crystal clear, the visions come with much greater clarity. It's the place where we begin to be future oriented instead of looking at the past.

And this one is really key for today. It's the place where end-time revelation is suddenly unsealed right in front of you.

That is the experience the apostle John received. John begins the description of his experience with an unusual phrase: *"After these things I looked..."*

Like the apostle John, we really need to get to the "after these things" part. Where we can look, we can see, and we can know things with certainty.

The next verse says, *"Immediately I was in the spirit. And behold a throne..."* From where I sit this is what is opening to us in 2022. The door is open, and we are being called up higher to see, to hear, and to interact more intimately with our Lord. It says He will show us things! Our entire walk so far has been for this season. I declare we are there, and it is going to be the most amazing season. But first we need to repent and cleanse ourselves from past traumas and disappointments. We need to light the flame again!

> *Lord, forgive us where we have faltered and become sluggish. Ignite us with Your flame again. The flame that once consumed us. Ignite all those dry, tender places that need Your touch again. We want to burn for You like we once did. We need You more than ever; we are more empty than*

> *when we began this journey. Please fill us now with Your*
> *flame! Purify us. Purify our hearing, our visions, our love*
> *for You. Consume all other loves that keep us from You. Let*
> *us stand in the flame and be the trailblazers we are called*
> *to be. Let us be dressed and ready for service. We don't need*
> *You to serve us; we want to serve You with all our hearts.*
> *Let us hear Your voice, no matter how faint, and respond*
> *immediately. So immediately we can be in the Spirit, and*
> *behold Your throne!*

I just want to close this portion by emphasizing a key point. As Jon has shared throughout the book, the Lord is unsealing scrolls of revelation meant for the end-time Church.

Remember the admonition to Daniel as he was receiving scrolls of revelation. *"But as for you, Daniel, keep these words secret and seal up the book (scrolls) until the end of time"* (Dan. 12:4).

As of 2022, we are at a point where the door is open NOW in a way it has not been before to see God's scrolls unsealed, and His decrees released.

And with this opportunity also comes an unveiling of the Author of these scrolls, the Ancient of Days. Below is yet another confirmation for you on this. A door now stands open.

The Door to Daniel 7

On August 22, 2005 the Lord gave me a similar prophetic experience to Jolene regarding an open door. This dream clearly communicated God's requirement for the door to become opened. Note that the open door was an invitation to gain revelation from a chapter I was barely familiar with at the time, but that has come to define many of our pursuits ever since, including this book.

> Please fill us now with
> Your flame! Purify us.
> Purify our hearing, our
> visions, our love for You.
> Consume all other loves
> that keep us from You.
> Let us stand in the flame
> and be the trailblazers
> we are called to be.

I was walking down a cobblestone path at twilight. A single path forked into two paths. One veered to the left and the other to the right. Standing at the crossroads, both paths seemed to dead-end at the face of a huge cliff. Looking closer, I saw that there was a door embedded into the cliff at the end of each path.

I had come to a place of decision. I knew intuitively that the choices made now would significantly determine our direction for the future, and that U-turns were not really an option. It was as though the momentum of each path would somehow sweep us in.

It's very important to understand the options before me were in no way representing "left or right" from a political worldview. The path to the right represented a direction which seemingly led to a life of ease and provision, a shortcut to what many perceive as the American Dream. In my spirit I knew the personal rewards would seem great, but that the true impact for the Kingdom would be small.

The Lord showed me that the path to the left was much more difficult, but led to the fulfillment of His dream for me. This path would have the greatest impact upon society for the Kingdom. I somehow knew that on the other side of the door was Daniel 7.

Thinking at this time of decision, there was a magnetic pull to take the easy way, the way I thought was right. My path in Christ at that time had brought me through hardships I never could have imagined. Maybe this was an invitation to life as a "veteran of war" instead of remaining in the battle. Maybe this was actually His will.

Praying at this time of decision, I felt a small tug to turn toward the door to Daniel 7. In fact, my feet started walking before my mind was made up! As I walked along the path, still struggling to know if this was God's will for me, the Lord flashed a proverb across my mind. *"There is a way that seems RIGHT to a man, but the end thereof is DEATH"* (Prov. 14:12, emphasis added).

The Kingdom Path

Many of you are at a similar point of decision right now. The Kingdom path is not the path of least resistance—far from it. But it is the path of life. Those who seek to save their lives will lose it, while those who lose their lives for His sake and the Gospel will find it.

The Lord also showed me that the path to the left wasn't truly to the left—it was actually the straight path! The path wasn't warped, but my perspective was. *My unhealed, unredeemed perspective made the wrong way look right.*

The leading of the Holy Spirit can sometimes be confused with the voice of our own wounding, or even our own strength. Let's ask Holy Spirit to continually show us the path that we're on, and the path He wants us to take.

The 222 Sword

In the vision, with the door ahead of me, I saw a large sword lying on the cobblestones. The word *FAVOR* was engraved on the front of the sword, and the number "222" was on the back.

Seeing the sword, my first thought was, *This vision is like a video game. Pick up the sword, tap the door, and go through.*

Though my strategy was set, the Lord was about to show that this was not a game. As I leaned over to pick up the sword, Holy Spirit spoke: *NO.* The authority and urgency of the word literally imparted the fear of God. Then, very firmly in my spirit came the words, *This sword will only be given in exchange for your time.*

Friends the imagery of the "222 sword" was important in 2005. But it means vastly more, and is vastly more important right now in 2022 than I could ever have imagined. God is offering an Isaiah 22:22 key that opens the door to Daniel 7, and a weapon of war needful to turn the battle!

Lynnie Harlow had a dream where I was turning a battle of the American Revolution. I believe the "222 sword" represents the weapon of war given for us to gain this new ground.

Sword for Your Time

I began to understand here what made this path so difficult. God wasn't first concerned about redeeming process on this walk, but *redeeming intimacy with Him.* He wanted my time.

Many who receive a prophetic decree focus so intently on the direction of the word, or its ultimate result, that we completely miss the built-in mandate of relating with Him to see the word fulfilled. Receiving prophetic vision then becomes like a video game. We run flippantly from word to word, enjoying the experience but never giving time for the word of His heart to penetrate our hearts and take root.

In this hour, new weapons of war are being released to the Body of Christ. The Lord invites you to give your time in exchange for the sword of His Word. To sanctify your time to Jesus, and allow Him to structure and steward it as He desires. Be willing to change course as the Spirit leads you. *"My times are in your hands!"* (Ps. 31:15).

With sword in hand, God is opening to us the door to Daniel 7. It is a sword of favor and Isaiah 22:22 authority. Let's all claim this for the new season.

Note that Daniel was watching by night in Babylon when the Lord began to dramatically unveil His throne-room activities. He watched in the Spirit and literally prophesied the most significant events of the end times. As Jolene so powerfully shared, this door is opening for you. Wait on the Lord. We have entered a season where there is "weight in the wait." The Lord is releasing a supernatural anointing to make known the mysteries of God, even in the midst of your Babylon.

> In this hour, new weapons of war are being released to the Body of Christ. The Lord invites you to give your time in exchange for the sword of His Word.

Making Covenant at Your Threshold

We want you to experience the fullness of the windows of opportunity He is opening. For this to occur, we encourage you to establish covenant with Christ personally over your gateways.

Remember that God is sevening your 22s in this season. Invite Him into covenant with you at the thresholds or gateways now opening before you. Time Gates. New homes. Open doors for new opportunities. And especially the gateways of your relationship with Him. He is beckoning you and me to make a threshold covenant.

The subject of threshold covenants was covered at length in chapter 15 of our companion book *White House Watchmen*. Here is a brief summary, taken directly from the chapter.

The book of Exodus shows how, in an unprecedented display of power, a subjugated people experienced God's hand of deliverance from Egypt. The Red Sea parted. They crossed the threshold and escaped four hundred years of slavery and death. The sea then flooded the pathway again to provide a barrier between Israel and her enemies—and a point of no return for the Jewish people.

Then during a dramatic Passover exactly forty years later, a threshold opened up again. This time the waters of the Jordan parted. Joshua, or Yeshua in Hebrew, led His Covenant People across to the Promised Land. Note that from the time the Jews were sheltered in place, and the blood of the Lamb was placed on the thresholds of their homes, every other threshold they encountered gave way to them.

Most of us have wrongly learned one of the most important aspects of Passover. Since we were kids, we've been taught that the blood of the Lamb was applied to protect homes and families *from the Lord* as He entered the land of Egypt. Our expectations have therefore been programmed to apply the blood as a barrier which ultimately protects us from God.

Actually the truth is quite the opposite. The Jews were invited to enter into a "threshold covenant" at Passover not to distance themselves from God, but to invite His presence to enter their homes and protect them. An ancient protocol had been followed whereby the invited Guest was actually welcomed across the thresholds of their homes.

Covenant unlocks glory. And from the beginning, the Passover meal was given by God first as a protocol to welcome Him in!

Archeological finds prove that threshold covenants were commonplace long before the Jews were freed from Egypt. In other words, it was already customary, familiar language. Bridegrooms and brides established threshold covenants, even placing blood on the doorposts of their homes. Sovereigns were welcomed into dwellings with sacrifices for their feast prepared at the gateways of their hosts. Blood from the meat would be applied on the doorposts as a protocol display of invitation and honor.

"In dealing with his chosen people, God did not invent a new rite or ceremonial at every stage of his progressive revelation to them," Trumbull writes. "But he took a rite with which they were already familiar, and gave to it a new and deeper significance in its new use and relations." Trumbull continues, "And now Jehovah announced that he was to visit Egypt on a designated night, and that those who would welcome him should prepare a threshold covenant, or a pass-over sacrifice, as a proof of that welcome; for where no such welcome was made ready for him by a family, he must count the household as his enemy."[1]

That's astonishing, isn't it? "Yet isn't it just like God, in His nature and character of love, to provide the very covenant meal by which He is welcomed to enter into our lives"—and into the gateways He is opening for us. "The blood is applied. The presence is welcomed.... And from this moment of covenant, every other threshold you encounter must give way."[2]

Friends, a door stands open for you and me. Let's meet the Lord at the threshold, and invite Him to move with us across the threshold, and into the new season of revelation and fulfillment.

Turnaround Decree 9: Threshold Covenant

Father God, by faith I stand at the threshold of this open door and invite You by covenant to enter and encounter me. As requested, I consecrate to you my time gates—my chronological time, as well as the kairos times, the windows of opportunity you are setting before me. Please grant me Your keys of authority and favor in exchange.

Father, I consecrate to You all physical gateways in my stewardship. I also consecrate to You all of the spiritual gateways in my stewardship. Thank You for the open door You have set for me to come up higher and join with You! Thank you for also coming through the open door into my domain. With all my heart I welcome You to come abide with me.

By faith I receive the body and blood of Jesus for the remission of my sins, and the establishment of Your threshold covenant with me. I apply the blood of Jesus, and the Body of Jesus over all of these gates to consecrate them to You, and welcome You through. Thank You for also welcoming me through to interact with You, and Your eternal throne. I decree these thresholds now become places of encounter, of new beginnings, of protection and provision from You and revelation from Your heart.

According to Exodus 23:20 I ask that You now send Your angel before me to guard me along the path and to bring me into the place which You have prepared. Secure the new way forward! In Jesus' Name. Amen.

CHAPTER 10

THE CONFLICT
OF COVENANTS

"But you have come to Mount Zion and to the city of the living God, the heavenly Jerusalem, and to myriads of angels, to the general assembly and church of the firstborn who are enrolled in heaven, and to God, the Judge of all, and to the spirits of the righteous made perfect, and to Jesus, the mediator of a new covenant" (Hebrews 12:22-24).

IN 2001, ON A BRIGHT NIGHT on the Standing Rock reservation, apostolic leader Jay Swallow paced restlessly beneath a star-laden sky. Elders of the Sioux tribe had called for the Native American leader to help break the cycle of monthly suicides overtaking many young adults. Neither counseling, coaching, or clamping down had abated the monthly occurrences. In fact, grief over loss had only multiplied the victims.

The Lord had shown Jay that the Baal principality was behind the atrocities. In fact, this biblical foe was in his mind the preeminent "strongman" afflicting both Native America and the United States. Biblical correlations to the principality were clear, especially the blood-letting pictured as an act of worship during the days of Elijah.

In any case, Jay knew it had to be bound. But over many days of ministry, the breakthrough he had come to attain seemed as distant as the prairie's darkened horizon.

Suddenly a bright light appeared.

Jay stood still, but the light moved. A plane? A comet? Maybe a missile? The US Navy veteran knew too well of the thermonuclear silos in the region. God forbid the ultimate suicide was at hand.

Amazingly, the light drew closer.

Jay looked within himself, his spirit stirring. Somehow this brightness in the sky was from God.

The bright light slowed, then hovered. A scroll burst from the center, and then the light itself became the scroll that unfurled before him. On it was written one line of simple instruction. "Bind the principality behind the suicides over to the Court of Heaven." A jury was to be convened, and a verdict rendered in favor of the saints.

Following the scroll's instructions, Jay convened a jury of tribal leaders. He bound the principality Baal over to the Court of Heaven. The leaders together presented their case. Judgment was rendered.

And the cycle of suicides literally stopped on a dime.

Soon after, Jay Swallow worked with his covenant friend apostle John Benefiel to develop the scroll's contents for application on a broader level. The Divorce Decree from Baal was the result. And with Native American apostolic authority, they initiated what soon became the largest and most comprehensive repudiation of idolatry in American history.

The decree was prayed through onsite at more than 20,000 occult altars across the nation, including every Masonic lodge, every abortion clinic, virtually every known occult altar, and more. Soon breakthroughs similar to what Jay experienced at Standing Rock began to burst forth concurrently across the nation. Droughts broke. Economic decline turned around. Salvations increased dramatically. And even elections began to shift.

In both scope and magnitude of results, the Divorce Decree from Baal has become a modern prototype of a successful turnaround decree in our nation. It has now gone global.

The story behind the Divorce Decree from Baal is well known in prayer circles. But what's barely even perceived is that Jay Swallow, as an apostolic father to his people, was contending with everything in him for the lives of his children. It was then that breakthrough was decreed from the throne. The lives of countless young ones were preserved. In a very real way, a new birth of freedom was granted.

> Jay Swallow, as an apostolic father to his people, was contending with everything in him for the lives of his children. It was then that breakthrough was decreed from the throne. The lives of countless young ones were preserved.

Darkness Shifts by Covenant

With the supernatural unfurling of Jay's scroll from Heaven came a new awareness of how to gain victory over the forces of darkness the Bible identifies as principalities and powers. Until Heaven's instructions accompanying the Divorce Decree from Baal were given, the primary approach to strategic-level spiritual warfare was simply to take authority over principalities through binding, loosing, and decreeing. This approach is inherently scriptural and has helped to initiate tremendous breakthroughs on a global level.

"Behold I give you authority to tread on serpents and scorpions, and OVERCOME ALL THE POWER of the enemy," Jesus admonished in Luke 10:19. *"Nothing shall by any means harm you."*

All means *all*. And I agree.

But one of the greatest mysteries consistently encountered by spiritual warriors is why many forces simply did not budge. In some cases, after initial territorial confrontations things actually got worse.

Fresh revelation regarding the power of covenant has helped clear up a lot of this mystery. Obviously, our faith is founded on covenant with God through Jesus Christ. What we initially failed to fully grasp is that principalities and powers were enthroned by covenants made with people as well. These covenants granted the enemy legal access to generational bloodlines of families, to businesses, communities and cultures, to nations, and even to governmental institutions. *"Bow your knee to me, and all this can be yours..."*

And very simply, to see freedom come, the pacts with darkness needed to be repudiated, the covenants annulled. Putting into practice the *Back to the Future* mandate on a societal level by repairing the past to redeem the present and secure God's dream for the future (see chapter 8).

This is why the Divorce Decree from Baal proved so effective. Very simply, Jay Swallow and John Benefiel were given clarity from the throne on how to see ancient and present-day covenants with the Baal principality annulled.

But it's important to note that both marriage and divorce are first matters of law. To obtain a divorce that annuls a marriage, you and your partner must receive a legal verdict from a judge. The findings of the verdict are administered to each party through a divorce decree. As noted in the previous chapter, this principle also applies to cleansing generational lines that have

America is in a conflict of covenants. Really the nations are. And the biggest prize being contended for by each side is actually our children.

been committed to the enemy. It applies to family lines, to spheres of authority, to regions and nations. We must renounce and replace!

The Conflict of Covenants

The stopping point here that stuns most Western Christians is that our societies are unduly influenced by covenants with the occult in similar way to third world nations.

It does not take a prophet to discern significant division is afflicting America right now. Most try to define it as Right versus Left. Really it's not. It's right versus wrong. And the polarization can best be understood by discerning covenantal alignment. Through word and action, many are being seduced into aligning with an antichrist spirit instead of with the Lord. The priorities and causes embraced by each side largely reflect this.

In short, America is in a conflict of covenants. Really the nations are. And the biggest prize being contended for by each side is actually our children.

Elijah's Secret Counsel

"As the Lord, the God of Israel lives, before whom I stand, there shall certainly be neither dew nor rain during these years, except by my word!" (1 Kings 17:1).

Elijah ruled by decree. His legacy must become our destiny today.

Note that the days in which Elijah lived are so similar to ours it's haunting. A parallel world in which the defining conflict is actually a conflict of covenants between Baal and the Lord.

In Elijah's day, there were essentially two thrones of governance over Israel operating at the same time: Elijah's and the one occupied by Ahab and Jezebel. Elijah's throne represented God's covenantal interests. The throne occupied by Ahab and Jezebel had become so corrupted by idolatry and covenant-breaking that it had essentially been given over to Baal.

Eventually, the throne of Elijah prevailed. It will in our day too.

In a similar way, as we have shared, two thrones have emerged in America. They are present in every aspect of society, but especially in the governmental realm, the financial realm, and the religious realm. On one hand we have Jezebel's table, and on the other we have the Table of the Lord.

Jezebel's table and the Table of the Lord both are altars of worship. They represent two opposing thrones of governance, two tables of provision, two seats of judgment, and two separate covenants, both sealed in blood. They are at the core two forms of payment for your soul.

Jezebel Thrones

The union of Ahab and Jezebel is very telling. Jezebel worshiped Baal. In fact, the name *Jezebel* means "married to Baal" or "Baal is my husband." She was from Assyria, the ancient seat of this dark power. The prophets of Baal ate at her table, even while the prophets of the Lord were persecuted. She infused all Israel with the ways of Baal worship, including the most heinous forms of sexual immorality as sacred acts of worship. Babies were sacrificed on altars to Baal. Temple prostitutes openly engaged Baal worshipers in their practices.

And their union forged an alliance of nations, essentially a transnational governmental structure, in which the covenant nation of Israel was forced to align with Assyria under the principality of Baal.

That's trouble.

Much like today's world, this covenant conflict was played out before the eyes of all the nation. Jezebel thought she had all of Israel under lockdown. She had usurped the very throne of God's Covenant Land, and all Israel had seemingly become subservient to her satanic spell.

And food sacrificed to these idols was received into the innermost parts of God's people. Note that the spirit of the idol was invoked into the sacrifice, so that when the food was consumed, practitioners believed that a demonic spirit was imparted.

But eating food sacrificed to idols meant more than just partaking of meat that had been ritually sacrificed. Jezebel was queen, and Jezebel's table was a supply line controlled by government. At a core level, eating food from Jezebel's table meant that God's own people had to compromise their consecration to God and their God-given values, personally and as a nation, simply to receive their daily bread.

Sound familiar? It should.

Remember the heritage of God's Covenant People. He had literally fought a revolution against Pharaoh, against the gods of Egypt and the government of Egypt, to free His people from the slavery and subservience that came from a government tied to idolatry.

God brought them into His Covenant Land—the only ground on earth He cut covenant with Himself to claim.

Covenants legally establish thrones of governance. God's dream was that He would rule with His people on Israel's seat of authority forever. But the leaders of Israel succumbed to idolatry, sexual depravity, and unholy alliances, literally yielding their thrones of governance by covenant over to Jezebel.

The Emergence of Elijah Thrones

Yet it is against this backdrop that the Lord unveiled Elijah the prophet. A man trained in secret by the Lord, hidden in the wilderness hills until God's chosen time for breakthrough. The name *Elijah* literally means "the Lord is God." I have to believe his time of hiddenness included great encounters and great purging, similar to those found in Zechariah 3, so that his character could become refined into a reflection of his God. This time of hiddenness prepared him for the season at hand. It was turnaround time.

Jezebel had her throne. But a throne was given to Elijah that no devil or government could challenge. *It was a throne established by covenant with God to bring His governance to His Covenant Land.* From this throne God brought discipline and also restoration.

Elijah's Secret Counsel

"As surely as the Lord God of Israel lives, before whom I stand, no rain nor dew all these years except at my word!"

That is such a bold statement. Note that Elijah's throne was connected to God's throne. It was essentially an outpost of the true King's throne on earth, joined together by covenant. And all he decreed came to pass.

What was Elijah's secret? Elijah stood in the council of the Lord. He received divine directives and decrees from the throne.

Did you know there is a secret council that meets regularly to determine the destinies of nations and peoples? It's true. What you've read about with the Illuminati, Masons, Davos, the Bilderbergs, Soros, and his cronies, etc. are but weak, corrupted imitations of the true ruling council. The council of God.

Beloved, the council of God ruled in the days of Elijah, as you can see. Daniel saw Heaven's council in action and described it for us. An even greater glimpse into the domain of this council has been given by the apostle John, as conveyed by the elders seated before the throne. And the Lord wants us to participate in it.

Many have previously taught about the exclusivity of this council, that it is essentially reserved for a chosen few. I personally believe that as with most of God's revealed governmental structures, there are levels to this council, and to our participation in it.

But in Jeremiah 23:9-22, one of the greatest chapters on the council of God in all the Bible, the prophets are rebuked for *not* participating in the council. Read this passage very, very carefully. The references I want you to linger on are at the end.

As for the prophets: My heart is broken within me, all my bones tremble; I have become like a drunken man, and like a man overcome by wine, because of the Lord and because of His holy words. For the land is full of adulterers; for the land mourns because of the curse. The pastures of the wilderness have dried up. Their course is evil and their might is not right. "For both prophet and priest are defiled; even in My house I have found their wickedness," declares the Lord.... "Moreover, among the prophets of Samaria I saw an offensive thing: they prophesied by Baal and led My people Israel astray." Also among the prophets of

Jezebel had her throne. But a throne was given to Elijah that no devil or government could challenge.

231

Jerusalem I have seen a horrible thing: the committing of adultery and walking in deceit; and they strengthen the hands of evildoers, so that no one has turned back from his wickedness. All of them have become to Me like Sodom, and her inhabitants like Gomorrah...

This is what the Lord of armies says concerning the prophets: "Do not listen to the words of the prophets who are prophesying to you. They are leading you into futility; they tell a vision of their own imagination, not from the mouth of the Lord. They keep saying to those who despise Me, 'The Lord has said, "You will have peace"'; and as for everyone who walks in the stubbornness of his own heart, they say, 'Disaster will not come on you.' But who has stood in the council of the Lord, that he should see and hear His word? Who has paid attention to His word and listened?...

I did not send these prophets, but they ran. I did not speak to them, but they prophesied.

But if they had stood in My council, then they would have announced My words to My people, and would have turned them back from their evil way, and from the evil of their deeds."

Elijah stood in the council of God. He turned a nation back to the Lord. Likewise God promises that those who will stand in His council in this hour will receive an anointing to turn God's people back from the evil of their way, and from the evil of their deeds.

Turnaround. Or in Hebrew, *teshuvah*. It is given to those who dare, who refuse to be refused. Stand in His council! Participate in His rulership. We explored with you the throne room verdict from Daniel 7:22 and the extraordinary turnarounds that followed. In this chapter we shared the profound example of apostolic father Jay Swallow, who gained Heaven's counsel to overcome forces taking out the children of his tribe. I'm just sayin'... This is happening today. Dare to receive your counsel from Heaven's council, and decree what He is decreeing. You will also see God's turnaround released!

Turning the Hearts of this Generation

"Behold, I am going to send you Elijah the prophet before the coming of the great and terrible day of the Lord. He will turn the hearts of the fathers back to their children and the hearts of the children to their fathers, so that I will not come and strike the land with complete destruction" (Malachi 4:6).

Altars are built to bear witness to covenant. Elijah repaired the altar of the Lord. By this, symbolically he repaired God's covenant with the Lord, which had been cast down. He then called upon God to move by His Spirit. "O Lord, send Your fire," Elijah cried, "that this people may know that You are God, and that You have turned their hearts back to You!"

The fire fell. And a nation was turned back to the Lord.

It is in this context that Malachi prophesies and end-time release of the Elijah anointing, with a focus on turning the hearts of the fathers back to the children, and the children to the fathers. Please understand it's the same anointing. And it's gained first by standing before the Lord.

You and I are invited to pioneer this dimension of the Elijah anointing today. That's what "Turnaround Tuesday" is all about. Family restoration is at the core of the move of God's Spirit prophesied for the end times! God wants to win the hearts of this generation. And in context, a nation will turn.

Heaven's Decree—Progression from Release to Fulfillment

Again, many times when a decree is released there is a process involved in seeing it fulfilled. That is not always the case. Countless times we have seen immediate manifestations. But especially with decrees that impact spheres of society, there is often a progression from release to fulfillment in which your sustained engagement is needed.

With that, let's return to the heavenly scroll given in a midnight hour to Jay Swallow called the Divorce Decree from Baal. It is perhaps the best example I know that shows the process involved in seeing a decree through to manifestation.

First, there was a birth, a release of the decree. As we've already chronicled, this release came largely in private, in the midst of a midnight cry for help on a Native American reservation in the Dakota wilderness. Instructions were given on how to immediately implement the parameters of the decree in order to see an initial fulfillment. But the Lord had much more in mind.

Second, the private movement surrounding the decree became trumpeted on a global level through a massive stadium event. The Call Nashville was held on 07-07-07. Hosted by Lou Engle, the event was focused on releasing the decree to the Body of Christ to divorce Baal—in other words, divorce historic and present idolatry—and renew covenant with the Lord.

I believe the Call Nashville will go down in history as one of the most pivotal for America and the world. The trumpet sounded. It was God's chosen moment to release the decree, and in process it forever changed the face of apostolic Christianity on a global basis.

Dutch Sheets spoke on overcoming Baal as the "strongman" of the nation. Mike Bickle shared on the movement of the heart conveyed in

Hosea 2 from Baal to Jesus. James Goll shared on the potential embedded within this mandate for Nashville, for America as a whole, and for Israel.

And John Benefiel and Jay Swallow shared extraordinary results they had already gained from repudiating covenants with Baal. Through the trumpeting of these voices and more, the mandate burst forth from the Call movement to the nations of the earth. Return to covenant with the Lord, divorced from our idolatry.

This was followed through with a declaration of our divorce from Baal as a nation, and restoration of covenant with Him.

It's really important to note that the Call Nashville on 07-07-07 was not an end in itself, but a gateway by which the mandate to divorce Baal was globally launched. It was essentially a beautiful engagement ceremony in which the invitation to be married to Jesus was given, and clear parameters set. But it was not the wedding itself.

The marriage covenant unites a bridegroom and a bride who have discovered a sustained expression of love, of passion and mutual affection to the extent that neither desires to exist separately, only together, forsaking all others. It is first, of course, a legal contract. In the same manner a decree of divorce represents a desired intention to dissolve a marital relationship. But it is also a legal contract. And in both cases, the judgment of a court must be secured for the intended result to have legal standing.

And soon after this gathering, to gain the honor for the nation of America to genuinely be married to the Lord, divorced from historic idolatry, very specific actions made clear by Heaven's Court to satisfy the legal requirements by which the divorce decree could be genuinely granted. In this case, the mandate given by the Court was to divorce Baal onsite at every altar of historic or present idolatry in the nation, including Masonic lodges and temples, abortion clinics, all known occult altars, and so much more.

For this process, a divorce decree was actually written in which all covenants with Baal were renounced and repudiated, and Heaven's Court was approached to grant the request of divorce as well as the issuance of a restraining order against the principality. Under the leadership of apostle John Benefiel with Cindy Jacobs and others, this divorce decree was declared onsite at more than 20,000 altars of idolatry in every state of America.

To our knowledge the effort to divorce Baal became the largest and most comprehensive repudiation of idolatry in American history.

Seven Steps to Manifesting Kingdom Decrees

Remember, we are following the progression of a decree from Heaven from initial release to fulfillment. Let's look at the process so far.

1. The conception, or initial private receiving, of a Kingdom decree.

2. The announcement of the decree into the spheres it will impact as well as teaching that expands the understanding of the broader Body of Christ.

3. Stewardship of the decree through prayer and Spirit-directed engagement to prepare the way for its fulfillment. This includes following through with repentance and other directives that satisfy the requirements of Heaven's Court regarding the issues being dealt with.

4. The Issachar alert that the time of fulfillment has come.

5. Birthing intercession surrounding the release.

6. The "finishing decree." Declaring again the Kingdom decree, this time with a governmental anointing, also referred to as a breaker anointing, to release immediate and sustained results.

7. The manifestation of the Kingdom decree. Remember that the Breaker brings *forced compliance* with the Kingdom decree.

In regards to the decree of divorce from Baal, the fulfillment came in an incredibly unique way. And it set the course for the issuance of the Daniel 7:22 verdict of justice in favor of the saints, along with the extraordinary turnarounds that followed. I want to emphasize again, by decree of Heaven's Court, the turnaround movement has now been reconstituted and rereleased. If past experience proves true, the impact for the Kingdom will be even greater.

The project to divorce Baal began in December 2009. And by July 2011, the nationwide mandate had largely been fulfilled. Jolene and I, along with Abby Abildness, hosted an event in Washington, DC, on July 4, 2011, to present to the Lord the completed work, and request from Him the corresponding promise that the divorcement from Baal and restoration of the marriage covenant with our nation be fully granted.

Remember one of the meanings of the name "Baal" is taskmaster, or slavemaster. It's why all subjugation and slavery is sourced from idolatry. And God was granting our freedom! To me there is no greater monument to freedom from subjugation than the Lincoln Memorial in Washington, DC.

For this reason we gathered there for this covenant reset on July 4. We were joined by apostle John Benefiel, Negiel Bigpond, Harry Jackson, and many leaders from across the nation. We together asked the Lord to grant a verdict of justice in our favor, sealing the divorce.

We then presented the Lord with a Declaration of Covenant, reminding Him of our covenantal foundations and asking for His hand in marriage again. The content of this Declaration on July 4, 2011, largely framed the Mayflower Covenant Renewal, presented to the Lord on 11-11, 2020.

We gave the Lord one more request. Rick Ridings, who with his wife, Patricia, directs Succat Hallel in Jerusalem, had received a vision a decade earlier that we felt applied to the ceremony. He saw Washington, DC, encompassed by a hard shell of demonic resistance. Suddenly a divine "nutcracker" appeared and cracked this hard shell. Rick knew the shell represented the grip on our government by the strongman.

As we stood on the steps of the Lincoln Memorial, facing the Washington Monument and the Capitol farther on, our combined plea was very simple. *Lord, crack that nut! As a sign that You have heard us, and that You have granted our request, crack hard shell of demonic resistance.*

Would you believe that exactly 50 days later, an unprecedented regional earthquake rocked Washington, DC? The quake, measuring 5.8 on the Richter scale, actually cracked the Washington Monument!

Gargoyles toppled from the National Cathedral. And even a primary altar to Baal on a national and international level was affected. The roof cracked, and the altar was damaged to the extent that a year later it was still roped off.

Can't make this stuff up. In a way only God could orchestrate, the covenant restoration divorced from Baal was confirmed. A new birth of freedom was concurrently released. And

> Covenant restoration is at the heart of God's move both in families and in the nation. It's actually a primary catalyst of the prophesied restoration. Covenant imparts identity. And it unlocks the power of God to restore, heal, and bring deliverance.

the date marking America's independence has now become the anniversary of His covenant restoration.

Beloved, maybe it's not coincidence that the Lord initiated the book Turnaround Decrees on July 4, 2021, exactly one decade later, with a vision of a simple scroll. God remembers! I cannot emphasize this enough. And as you remain faithful to the vision He has given you to decree and steward, you will see His extraordinary faithfulness in bringing it to pass.

Deliverance by Covenant

Covenant restoration is at the heart of God's move both in families and in the nation. It's actually a primary catalyst of the prophesied restoration. Covenant imparts identity. And it unlocks the power of God to restore, heal, and bring deliverance.

Did you know that God promises deliverance from the hand of every adversary? He does—in context with covenant.

> *"The covenant that I have made with you, you shall not forget, nor shall you fear other gods. But you shall fear the Lord your God; and He will save you from the hand of all your enemies"* (2 Kings 17:38-9).

This is no small promise. If you're like me, you probably have a list of enemies needing vanquished! So if ever there was a verse to align with, internalize, and decree, this is it. Covenant with God divorced from idolatry is God's requirement. The release of the very hand of the Lord to accomplish your deliverance is the promise, activated by decreeing! Here are seven steps to secure His deliverance.

1. Align with God's covenant.

2. Declare the decree of the Lord. Deliverance from the hand of every enemy!

3. Request the activation of His hand.

4. Pray in the Spirit over your situation.

5. Check your giving. God promises are activated in context with obedience to the divine exchange of tithes and offerings. This is a primary aspect of covenant alignment and yet, again, it is so often overlooked.

6. Ask the Lord to reveal any further issues needing settled on your part.

7. Don't attempt your own deliverance. Leave it in His hands, and be led by His Spirit into the deliverance that defines your future.

Given the potential of this promise, you'd think it would be plastered on every Sunday morning PowerPoint screen by now, and certainly every grandma's refrigerator. Instead it has been hidden, largely obscured through the ages. The reason? Maybe because the promise is directly correlated to an overall rebuke against Israel's idolatry.

The overall message of the passage is that God was actually pronouncing judgment after the people had embraced Baal and forsaken Him. The promise in context was merely a reminder of what should have been.

And that's a warning to us all.

> *"They rejected His statutes and His covenant that He had made with their fathers, and His testimonies which He had testified against them; they followed idols, became idolaters, and went after the nations... So they left all the commandments of the Lord their God...and served Baal. And they*

caused their sons and daughters to pass through the fire, practiced witchcraft and soothsaying, and sold themselves to do evil in the sight of the Lord, to provoke Him to anger."

The verse immediately following God's promised deliverance is perhaps the saddest in the Bible, given the potential they had just been offered.

"However they did not obey, but they followed their former rituals. So these nations feared the Lord, yet served their carved images; also their children and their children's children have continued doing as their fathers did, even to this day."

They feared the Lord, yet served their idols. Despite many breakthroughs, this sentiment still largely describes American culture today. Clearly the conflict of covenant continues. We're going to complete the turnaround. Vast multitudes are going to disengage from Jezebel's table and return to the table of the Lord, the table of His covenant. They are going to feast on His goodness! That said, as in the days of Elijah, there is much more work to be done.

Below is the Divorce Decree from Baal. It again originated with a scroll from Heaven given to Jay Swallow as he contended over the destinies of native children. In 2018 I had the privilege of writing a revision that further empowers this focus.

Turnaround Decree 10: Divorce Decree From Baal (Revised)

THE HIGHEST COURT IN THE KINGDOM OF GOD

IN RE THE MARRIAGE OF:

THE PEOPLE OF GOD

Plaintiff,

vs.

THE PRINCIPALITY OF BAAL

(Incl. Baal, Queen of Heaven, Leviathan)

Defendant

DECREE OF DIVORCE[1]

This matter comes on for hearing before the Supreme Judge of the Highest Court of the Kingdom of God on the petition of The People of God seeking a Decree of Divorce from the Principality of Baal, the Defendant in this matter (see Hosea 2).

The Court finds:

1. The Plaintiff's sins are forgiven. The Court recognizes the Plaintiff's request that this petition be rendered in favor of the people of God based upon this Court's previous precedent granting the remission of all sins through Jesus Christ. The Court recognizes the Plaintiff is an ambassador of Christ, stewarding His gift of righteousness and the ministry of reconciliation, reconciling, and restoring the world to favor with God (see John 20:23, 2 Cor. 5:18-20, Rom. 5:17).

2. The Plaintiff's assertions are fully substantiated: a. That this marriage was entered into by the Plaintiff based on lies and deceit by the Defendant, and b. That Plaintiff relied on fraudulent inducements and enticements by the Defendant, which Defendant had neither the intention or ability to deliver.

3. The Plaintiff renounces any and all right, claim, or interest in any possession jointly acquired with the Defendant during this Marriage, and that Plaintiff is entitled to have sole right, claim, and interest, in and to all the gifts, possessions and inheritance from Plaintiff's Father, and the Defendant is to be (now) and forever barred from the title, control, or use of any such gifts, possessions, or inheritance.

4. The Plaintiff repudiates any and all joint claims with the Defendant, and requests this court to sever all relationships with the Defendant of any nature, however and whenever such occurred, and seeks enforcement by this Court of Plaintiff's desire to be known by no other name than that given by Plaintiff's Father.

5. All offspring of this marriage are released into the sole jurisdiction of this Court, effective immediately. The Defendant's request for either sole or joint custody is denied. As per the Plaintiff's request, all claims by the Defendant to their lives and bloodlines are rescinded.

6. The Plaintiff also seeks an everlasting restraining order against the Defendant so as to keep the Defendant away from all persons or property belonging to the Plaintiff.

7. The Plaintiff seeks perpetual enforcement of this requested judgment in favor of the saints, restraining the enemy and releasing the saints to possess the Kingdom (see Dan. 7:22).

THE JUDGEMENT

WHEREFORE, this Court being fully advised in the evidence does find for the Plaintiff and against the Defendant in all matters material to the Plaintiff's Petition of Divorce, and does by this decree grant the Plaintiff a Divorce and all requests set forth above. That being the Order of this Court, from and after this date, so shall it be.

THE SUPREME JUDGE

SEVEN ON A SCROLL:
Manifesting Kingdom Decrees

Remember we are following the progression of a decree from Heaven from initial release to fulfillment. Let's take a look at the process.

1. The conception, or initial private receiving, of a Kingdom decree.

2. The announcement of the decree into the spheres it will impact as well as teaching that expands the understanding of the broader Body of Christ.

3. Stewardship of the decree through prayer and Spirit-directed engagement to prepare the way for its fulfillment. This includes following through with repentance and other directives that satisfy the requirements of Heaven's Court regarding the issues being dealt with.

4. The Issachar alert that the time of fulfillment has come.

5. Birthing intercession surrounding the release.

6. The "finishing decree." Declaring again the Kingdom decree, this time with a governmental anointing, also referred to as a breaker anointing, to release immediate and sustained results.

7. The manifestation of the Kingdom decree. (Note that the Breaker brings *forced compliance* with the Kingdom decree.)

CHAPTER 11

DIVORCING BABYLON

"The challenges of the hour do not mean you've failed. It means there's a dimension of punishment reserved for the Baal principality until this hour. The challenges correspond to the unlocking of this dimension."
—Word to Jon, January 2022

BY AND LARGE, GOD'S PEOPLE are no longer sitting around worshiping wooden idols, absorbing the influence of demonic powers represented by unsightly sculptures. But don't think for a moment our culture has moved beyond hard-core idolatry.

Our forefathers may have become captivated by a beast in a block of wood. Whereas the ancients were rebuked for tolerating Jezebel, today many today take into the depths of their beings movies, video games, music, internet, and now even metaverse expressions which showcase images of the beast. Pornography and the occult are joined at the hip and are rising in influence together. It astonishes me that Harry Potter and an unrestricted internet both remain celebrated babysitters to many children, even in Christian families.

Needless to say, our children are being targeted. On a broader level, educational systems, and institutions, even many Christian schools and colleges, have become co-opted from the inside out to propagate the spirit and values of darkened humanism rather than even basic morality or even basic common sense. We experienced this firsthand. The challenges our son, Jonathan, succumbed to is my plumb line on this. In a moment we will share crucial aspects of Jonathan's breakthrough I have never publicly told. They are vital for breakthrough for your sons and daughters. I will say that high level spiritual warfare against the spirit of humanism led directly to our initial breakthrough, and it will for yours too.

Let my children go!

We can't let down in this war. Even more importantly, we must realize how idolatry—in other words, the occult—is a major root of the primary systemic challenges America's parents are seeking to overcome. Over decades this influence has largely remained hidden, on purpose. But no more.

The book of Revelation prophesies that one day a mandate will come to worship the image of the beast and receive his mark as qualification for citizenship. The mark itself will probably include some kind of embedded computer chip that will function as a wallet for credit cards, as a tracking device, as a health monitor that also releases healing, as a connectivity modem, as a communication tool, and possibly even as an internal internet service that welcomes you into interactive realities projected on the screen of your own mind.

Most definitely it will also serve as a passport into the domain of a global governmental structure tied to idolatry, imposing its subjugation upon the masses. The technology for most of this is already here.

Many Christians are confused about their role, their next steps. Should we engage in culture, or just step back and let the, well, *chips* fall where they may?

Let me be very clear. If you've learned anything in this book, it is that you are in the Kingdom for such a time as this. Jesus invested His life to secure your salvation. He also redeemed your authority. You are called right now to reign in the earth! And reigning with Him now means partnering with Him to advance His Kingdom in your sphere. Even if there's a contending involved.

I believe "divorcing Babylon" is a clarion call both to the prayer movement and to the broader Body of Christ. The time is now to begin fulfilling the words of inscribed in both First Corinthians and, in direct reference to Babylon, the book of Revelation. *"'Come out from among them, and be separate,' says the Lord!"*

Baal Bows Down

Beginning with the reign of America's 45th president, Donald Trump, God began to strongly emphasize the calling of Cyrus as defined by Isaiah 45. Including freedom of religion, the exertion influence and authority, wealth generation, wealth accumulation, and the rise of governmental prophets in the excellence of Daniel. Further, the reign of Cyrus marked the beginning of the restoration movement which catalyzed freedom for God's people from Babylon and Persia.

In the reign of America's 46th president, Joe Biden, God is emphasizing Isaiah 46:1. *"Bel bows down, and Nebo stoops low!"*

Let me clarify what the Lord is speaking. During the reign of the 46th president, God's victory over Baal will be enforced at an even greater magnitude than before. Baal is going to be forced to bow. Nebo, the god of false prophecy, will also bow low as God's supremacy becomes further revealed. This is God's decree during Biden's reign! And we get to partner with it.

I love the New Living Translation of this passage.

> *"Bel and Nebo, the gods of Babylon, bow as they are lowered to the ground. They are being hauled away on ox carts. The poor beasts stagger under the weight. Both the idols and their owners are bowed down. The gods cannot protect the*

people, and the people cannot protect the gods. They go off into captivity together" (Isa. 46:1-2).

A companion passage to Isaiah 46:1 is Jeremiah 51:44.

"I will punish Bel in Babylon, and I will make what he has swallowed come out of his mouth; and the nations will no longer stream toward him. Even the wall of Babylon has fallen down!"

The Lord intends to punish Bel or Baal in Babylon—in other words, in the very midst of the Babylonian structure. Further, what this spirit and structure has stolen will be restored.

In context with these passages, the Lord recently spoke to me about the current state of America's government:

The challenges of the hour do not mean you've failed. It means there's a dimension of punishment reserved for the Baal principality until this hour. The challenges correspond to the unlocking of this dimension.

The light came on. Suddenly things began to make sense I believe the Lord is summoning us to fully realize this promise. It's time to divorce Babylon.

What Is Babylon?

According to Scripture, Babylon is a global, totalitarian governmental structure founded and perpetuated by covenants with antichrist spirits. The principality of Baal. Fallen angels. Satan himself. Scripture implies the melding of government, culture, science, technology, communication, intelligence, and global finance with this occult structure.

Babylon always attempts to overtake the Covenant Land. But Zion does not fall unless and until the Covenant People allow themselves to be seduced by Babylon's gods within the Covenant Land. The gates of sabotage are then open to succumb to Babylon's totalitarian dominion.

Babylon and Zion are both represented by geographic locations. But they are equally represented by thrones of rulership. These thrones connect the spiritual realm to the natural realm. Zion refers to an ancient region of Jerusalem where the original Tabernacle of David and Temple stood. But in the book of Hebrews, the apostle Paul makes clear to us that true Zion is actually the very throne of God.

> According to Scripture, Babylon is a global, totalitarian governmental structure founded and perpetuated by covenants with antichrist spirits.

"But you have come to Mount Zion and to the city of the living God, the heavenly Jerusalem, and to myriads of angels, to the general assembly and church of the firstborn who are enrolled in heaven, and to God, the Judge of all, and to the spirits of the righteous made perfect, and to Jesus, the mediator of a new covenant" (Hebrews 12:22-24).

Remember that covenants establish thrones of governance. In the spirit realm covenants open portals of access to either the Lord or forces of darkness. This fact can allow institutions, regions, and nations to become outposts of Babylon, or outposts of Zion.

Further, you and I can even become an outpost of Zion right in the midst of a Babylon throne. The greatest examples of this include the prophets Daniel and Elijah. Through Daniel's intercession, prophetic release, and high standard of virtue and loyalty, Babylon itself actually turned. And through Elijah's stand, the Babylonian influence interjected on the Covenant Land was restrained.

As we progress further down God's timetable, we will see clear examples of both Babylon thrones and Zion thrones over institutions, cities, states, and nations. Really they are already here. *But they can turn* if we follow Holy Spirit and implement His directives.

This brings us to a few defining points. The spirit and structure of Babylon is antichrist in nature. It is therefore anti-covenant, and tries to tear down the covenant relationship between God and His people. As a fruit of this, it is inherently anti-Semitic. Even if this aspect is initially cloaked, it's there beneath the surface.

And as an antichrist, anti-covenant stronghold it is also by nature anti-family. It targets your sons, your daughters, and mine to be sabotaged. Throughout history this has been no clearer than on the fields of battle contending over this very generation.

American Babylon or a Covenant Nation?

Trends in modern culture change with each passing breeze. But architectural trends do not bend so quickly. If a building bends with the wind, it won't last too long.

For this reason, architectural expressions in Washington, DC, are rarely trendsetters. Instead, most buildings have been thoughtfully constructed to invoke legacy and project subtle messages to the masses over many generations. Like the pillars of strength surrounding the Lincoln Memorial, venerating the people's president who rescued our nation from slavery. Or the deliberately undersized mansion called the White House, hosting the highest seat of authority in the land. The Museum of the Bible, with an architectural design that subtly evokes Noah's ark, is another example. Then there's the impenetrable layers of the Pentagon.

The newest landmark set to distinguish the Washington, DC, skyline is a bit more flamboyant. Strategically placed right across the street from the stoic Pentagon, the centerpiece of Amazon's HQ2 headquarters in Pentagon City is a ziggurat-shaped glass helix.

> Remember that covenants establish thrones of governance. This fact can allow institutions, regions, and nations to become outposts of Babylon, or outposts of Zion.

Provocatively, the coming structure dramatically resembles a rebuilt Tower of Babel.

You might remember the first Tower of Babel did not fare so well. Designed as a portal into the spirit realm, construction of the Tower was halted by God Himself. After personally evaluating the building's intentions and capabilities, he brought corresponding judgment. Capacities of universal communication, which once united all, suddenly failed. And humankind became scattered across the globe.

Prophetically, the rise of an intentional expression of the Tower of Babel in Washington, DC, brings two long-cultivated prospects into focus. First, forces of darkness are seeking turn God's Covenant Land into an expression of Babylon for this era. In other words, a global governmental structure uniting the world, sourced in a magnitude of idolatry often attributed to an antichrist spirit. Second, this unholy turnaround could eventually provoke God's judgment upon the land.

Perhaps this judgment has already begun. It has been said over and over again that the result of the 2020 election has been a blessing in disguise, because it has brought undeniable exposure to the depths to which our freedom governance has become co-corrupted. Or really, co-opted. Destructive motives of many leaders have been exposed. So have their covert alliances.

And what is generally termed "the deep state" has now been widely accepted as a real entity. A covert, elite subculture within government, diplomacy, the military, intelligence, media, finance, education, etc. Totalitarian and globalist in nature, the deep state seeks to impose its rulership on our land from the shadows, in open defiance of both constitutional boundaries and our Judeo-Christian foundations.

What unites these leaders? Babylon, essentially. Or the spirit of Babylon. It is the antithesis of the spirit of freedom through Jesus Christ. As a believer in Christ, you are the intercessor who stands between Babylon and the Covenant Land.

Your acquiescence is all the enemy needs. Let's give him no ground!

Covenant with Death and Hell Annulled

As a spiritual father to Israel, the prophet Isaiah confronted the deep state of his day with the following perceptions. First, governmental leaders come into covenant with occult powers, with death and hell, specifically to cover over their practices of corruption—to hide them from the people they are abusing instead of serving. These covenants are always sealed by the shedding of innocent blood.

Remember, the word *occult* means "hidden." Through covenants with demonic forces, a covering is established over these governmental leaders, basically an occult shield protecting them from being discovered.

Isaiah's second point is stunning. The Lord stands ready to annul these legal pacts with death and hell. That is His decree. The divorcement of Baal, explored in the previous chapter, is an example of a decree of annulment.

In Isaiah's own words:

> *Therefore, hear the word of the Lord, you scoffers,* **who rule this people** *who are in Jerusalem, because you have said, "We have made a covenant with death, and with Sheol we have made a pact. The gushing flood will not reach us when it passes by, because we have made falsehood our refuge and we have concealed ourselves with deception." Therefore this is what the Lord God says: "Behold, I am laying a stone in Zion, a tested stone, a precious cornerstone for the foundation, firmly placed. The one who believes in it will not be disturbed. I will make justice the measuring line and righteousness the level; then hail will sweep away the refuge of lies, and the waters will overflow the secret place. Your covenant with death will be canceled (annulled), and your pact with Sheol will not stand; when the gushing flood passes through, then you will become its trampling ground"* (Isaiah 28:14-18, emphasis mine).

I want to submit to you that, scripturally, a primary way by which God relieves the masses from the pharaoh-type governance tied to idolatry is by decrees that declare the annulment of covenants with death and hell which have empowered unrighteous leadership. They are legal transactions, secured by the Chief Cornerstone Jesus Christ through the investment of His own body and blood.

Strongholds—Shifting Both Spirit and Structure

The prospect of a rebuilt Tower of Babel in Washington, DC, is shocking. But occult architecture is nothing new to Washington, DC. According to their custom, many buildings have themselves become temples that invoke the presence of the deity being honored. They were designed and dedicated by covenant to achieve this very goal.

By their invocations, they are dedicating not just the buildings but the governmental seats of authority within them to the enemy. And that's not great news.

Let me give you a formula. **Spirit + structure = stronghold.** And by structure, I mean the altar of dedication, the systems, and the culture of a structure. Whether dealing with a lost daughter or a lost institution, to genuinely bring freedom from a stronghold we need to see both system and structure shift.

A great example of this is the Washington Monument. The structure is patterned after Egyptian obelisks fashioned as tributes to Osiris, the Egyptian god of the dead. Freemasons, who trace their spiritual heritage to the gods of Egypt and Babylon, constructed and dedicated the obelisk in what was once the geographic center of Washington, DC. They still consider it as the world's tallest Masonic lodge.

It's no coincidence that occultists from many different traditions gravitate to the monument to perform their rituals. Like the sorcerer we met on the Washington Mall just before the January 6 Capitol Storm. We had just finished praying, actually declaring the Mayflower Covenant Renewal, and were heading back when he stopped us and struck up a conversation. For some reason he wanted us to know we were not in the precise location where Osiris and her companion Isis were originally invoked. Private admission—that was on purpose. In any case, I have to wonder what role the activation of occult powers played on the disaster that ensued.

Anyway, freemasonry is widely attributed to opening the doors to every other expression of the occult and new age mysticism that has now gone mainstream in America. Again, their order was actually founded by an ancient union of Egyptian and Babylonian idolatry with worship of the living God, as a covert influence designed to dominate the world.

What is most important about freemasonry is not the fraternal order's viability or influence today. It is the fact that as a purported Christian institution it opened the gates to false religion and the occult. These seeds are being harvested now in both our culture and our generational lines.

And in a Babylonian kind of way, one of their essential doctrines is, "Many religions forming one altar to the Great Architect of the Universe." Which, according to their traditions is not God, but Lucifer. *"They loved God but served their idols..."*

Given this insight, it seemed to be even more a significant sign when the Washington Monument cracked in an earthquake exactly 50 days after we sought God's covenant renewal for Washington, DC, and the nation, divorced from Baal. When Heaven's Court was satisfied, it was almost as though the gavel of the Ancient of Days shook Washington, DC, as confirmation. Judgment in favor of the saints!

Not soon after, the largest and most comprehensive repudiation of national idolatry directly led to the largest and most comprehensive governmental turnarounds in modern American history. That's not hyperbole. Instead that's exactly what the Bible indicates *should happen* when His Covenant People wholeheartedly decree their repudiation of idolatry.

Now we are in a season of redemptive exposure, also prophesied in Isaiah 28.

The Fathering Movement Is a Freedom Movement

At the core, freemasonry and other occult structures serve as a false fathering movement that mentors each successive generation into the bondage of idolatry. Over centuries these hidden orders have served both to mentor and promote adherents into seats of authority and power.

Friends, it is no coincidence that the Lord is raising up a comprehensive, godly fathering movement in this hour. And just as Pharaoh of Egypt can represent the false fathering movement, so the true fathering movement being birthed today is at the core a freedom movement. A Moses movement. Really, a Jesus Movement!

Let My people go. Let My children go!

This movement marries the miracles of Exodus with the miracles of Acts as one new move of the Spirit for America and the nations. Great deliverance from subjugation will be joined by the restoration of God's governmental glory and the rapid advancement of the Church. Fresh revelation will burst forth. Holy conviction will sweep our communities. Pharaohs and pharaoh structures will come down. Healing will break forth. Many deliverances will be instantaneous, including freedom from various addictions. And it will happen on a massive scale.

Covenant restoration is at the core. It is really the missing piece to see the Lord gain breakthrough over the spirit, the structure, and the system of a stronghold.

The spiritually sensitive can already feel it in the atmosphere. You can breathe it in. You can literally taste and see the goodness of the Lord!

What's the next step? Here's the word of the Lord:

As the Body of Christ divorced Baal to mark the beginning of the new millennium, so we are being summoned now to divorce Babylon, both its spirit and structure. *Come out from among them, and be separate, says the Lord!*

And as we align with the Lord, we will see a dramatic turnaround.

Cough Up the Key!

Let me share with you just a few prophetic confirmations of this.

Remember Jeremiah 51:44: *"I will punish Bel in Babylon, and I will make what he has swallowed come out of his mouth; and the nations will no longer stream toward him. Even the wall of Babylon has fallen down!"*

The Lord intends to punish Bel or Baal in Babylon—in other words, in the very midst of the Babylonian structure. Further, what this spirit and structure has stolen will be restored.

Many years ago the Lord gave me an open vision where I was engaged in a wrestling match—against a sitting president of the United States. In the dream I threw the president down, climbed on top of him with my knees pinning him to the ground, and grabbed his throat. I shook him until he coughed up a key!

You have to understand my actions in the vision were completely opposite of my general demeanor and conduct. Scripture is clear that we don't wrestle against flesh and blood, but against principalities (see Eph. 6:12). I believe the sitting president in this dream represented the strongman of Baal over the White House. Certainly a Babylonian structure and worldview were imposed during this man's reign.

God is empowering us to win the wrestling match in the spirit in this hour. He is going to force the Baal principality to restore what he has swallowed. To cough up the keys of heritage and governmental authority that rightly belong to Him, and to His Eliakims.

> As the Body of Christ divorced Baal to mark the beginning of the new millennium, so we are being summoned now to divorce Babylon, both its spirit and structure.

That's the decree: Cough up the key!

Turnaround! Break the Snake, Free Your Children

You might be asking, what does all of this have to do with Turnaround Tuesday, or saving our children?

And the answer is, everything.

For cycles to break and genuine, lasting freedom to be gained, it's vital to move beyond the superficial. As John the Baptist declared, the axe must be laid to the root of the tree. Hacking relentlessly at the bad fruit hanging from the lowest branches might bring temporary satisfaction, especially when a primary purpose is relieving your own personal anger issues. But it never facilitates true change.

With this in mind, let's take another deep dive—quite literally into the belly of the beast. My son's salvation depended on the breakthrough I'm about to describe. Perhaps it is vital for your son and daughter as well. It's time for turnaround!

Remember the promise from Jeremiah 51:44: *"I will punish Bel in Babylon, and I will make what he has swallowed come out of his mouth."*

At our first Revolution conference in 2013, apostolic leader Rick Ridings shared an astonishing vision. A vile serpent, representing the spirit of humanism, had swallowed an entire generation. This spirit is merely another "face" or facet of the Baal principality, perceived earlier by Jay Swallow.

What astonished Jolene and me the most was that Rick saw the head and mouth over Massachusetts, the very state where my son Jonathan had graduated from college. In Rick's own words:

"I recently had a vision of an eagle circling over Philadelphia, who then swooped down to pull out a serpent which had been laced through thirteen original Colonies, and whose head and mouth were over Massachusetts. This serpent had swallowed a generation of young people into its belly, where they were trapped in deep darkness. I understood this serpent to be related to the sprit of the "Prince of Greece," of secular humanism, and it had especially swallowed young leaders attending East Coast Universities, and especially the Ivy League universities in the North East of America.

"As intercessors cried out, the eagle grabbed this serpent between its claws, took it up, and then ripped it apart, with this young generation released from the prison of its belly, and parachuting down on the East Coast to become points of burning fire in the darkness.

"I saw this dealing with this serpent had the potential, if guarded and fathered, of growing into a Third Great Awakening. At the same time, we can expect increasingly violent persecution to come from secular humanists against Christians, but if we persevere, it will only fuel great growth in this new move of the Lord upon this generation of young adults."

Our Revolution gatherings were actually launched with this focus. After Rick shared, he called for a symbolic prophetic action to release the turnaround decree that the spirit of humanism now release the captives in its belly. We saw how this spirit of humanism was essentially just another face of the Baal principality. We warred in the spirit. We then approached Heaven's Court and decreed the vision as Heaven's verdict over our children, asking for His verdict to be carried out with the Lord making war on their behalf. We declared the angelic hosts were released to catalyze this breakthrough as seen in the vision.

I'll never forget the moment the gavel fell. It set off tremors in the spirit realm which carried through in every way. It was just over a year later, on Christmas Day 2014, that we were led by the Spirit to begin our project called Turnaround Tuesday. And as you know, on Christmas Day, exactly a year from our launch, Jonathan was visited by the Lord Jesus Himself. Prison doors broke open. And a parachute had turned his free fall into a safe landing.

This is exactly what the Lord wants to do for your children. Again, it is essential to deal with the root, not just the branches or the low-hanging fruit.

Break the snake, free your children. Spirit of humanism, LET MY CHILDREN GO!

Restoring Inheritance—the Breaker Breaks Open

Another prophetic experience also comes to mind. Part of it was chronicled in our book *White House Watchmen*. But there's a portion of the vision I felt to withhold at the time. It now seems right to share it.

> The Breaker brings forced compliance with God's Kingdom decree.

In a dream in late June 2019, a woman representing the Jezebel spirit came before me. She looked sullen and defeated. Suddenly she started handing over car keys, house keys, bank accounts, title deeds to lands and inheritances, and more. I knew in the dream these possessions had been legally granted to me in a divorce settlement. But the woman, who again represented a Jezebel spirit, fiercely defied the order, and refused to let the acquisitions go. Therefore until that very moment, they had all remained in her possession.

In the dream I asked the woman, "What happened? What brought her seeming change of heart?" Her reply stunned me. Looking down, she simply said, "The Breaker breaks open."

The Breaker breaks open! That's another great decree. At that moment the Holy Spirit literally flooded my being with the entire Scripture: *"The Breaker goes up before them; they break out, pass through the gate and go out by it. So their king goes on before them, and the Lord at their head"* (Micah 2:13).

The Lord is moving as the Breaker in our midst. Remember, *the Breaker brings forced compliance to God's Kingdom decree*. What has been stolen and plundered from us and our domain will be restored to us. The Breaker breaks open!

Defending the Inheritance

The next part of the dream I've kept very private until now.[1]

I then dreamed I had taken possession of an old Christian campus on two hills. Beautiful, spacious grassy land. There was a large chapel or ministry center on the back hill and a newer community on the second hill that reminded me of an old camp meeting area, with cottages surrounding a tabernacle made of graying wood. Everything desperately needed renovation.

I knew in the dream we were vulnerable to attack. I was armed with a weapon. Jolene and I were in our "new" old home, one of the larger cottages located near the center. Somebody cut the lights. I told Jolene to call 911.

Men began pouring out of the chapel and moved toward the second hill. They seemed capable, rugged, and aggressive. It looked like an exodus. As the leader of the compound I began confronting them about weapons they were carrying, hidden in their coats and clothes. Daniel came from a nearby residence and engaged with them too. One by one they opened their coats and revealed shotguns and other weapons.

It seemed they were Christians by their language. But it also seemed clear they were planning an armed takeover of the entire campus, and that our lives and others were in severe danger.

"I did make this clear, right? And you did read the signs. No weapons on this campus!" I looked them straight in the eyes, one by one. "And who hit the Breaker to turn out the lights?"

The Breaker for the entire community was in the chapel, not the homes. One guy raised his hands. "Why did you do this?!" My inquiry was more an interrogation of him. His answer was full of religious language justifying his actions. But he admitted to cutting the lights.

Part of my reason for engaging the group was to stop them as a group from going any farther on the grounds, to make clear to them that we were resolved to protect our new inheritance. It worked. By the end the men seemed to be for us and respected our leadership over the property. They began to talk much more openly. A sheriff soon arrived from when Jolene had called 911. He backed us up.

I awoke.

What's the Interpretation?

Mountains often represent government. In retrospect, aspects of the second part of this dream may even reference the January 6 Capitol Storm, more than a year before it occurred. The White House could be symbolized by the chapel, where the march began, with Capitol Hill the camp meeting center. A major reason I consider this is because Daniel, the man who assisted me in the dream, is a Christian minister *who both lives and works on Capitol Hill.*

Probably the most important detail is that a circuit breaker at chapel, again perhaps symbolic of the White House, cut the power over the whole area. Lights out! According to Wikipedia, the basic function of a circuit breaker is to "interrupt current flow after protective relays detect a fault."

In a larger sense, the Breaker has been activated to enforce the decree restoring your inheritance. This includes His turnaround for families, businesses, ministries, properties, and covenant wealth. It also includes the restoration of apostolic covering and community. He will protect what He restores!

But in both cases a stand has to be taken for you to secure the inheritance God intends for you. Frustration with current conditions is provoking an exodus from debilitating structures to apostolic strongholds now under development. But the ground has to be possessed the right way, as directed by the Holy Spirit. Otherwise we may interrupt the flow of His power!

Let's move to some more good news—a final prophetic experience that will clearly convey to you the goal at hand as we engage in divorcing Babylon.

Earthquake! Babylon Falls, Covenant Nation Arises

It was early December 2021. We had just flown into Georgia from our home in Washington, DC, when I was awakened by the Lord at 4:00

a.m. I heard the Lord say, *As with Jacob you have wrestled with the Lord and prevailed!*

Immediately I saw a vision of America from a distance. I could see through the surface, even to the extent that the geological layers of the earth were visible. Suddenly the ground began to shake in an earthquake. Now most earthquakes are vertical, splitting the surface of the ground to the left and right. But this earthquake was internal, well beneath the surface, and it split the earth horizontally. Part of the earth ascended, and part of it descended.

I knew that what I was seeing in my vision was a covenant nation arising, and the deep state descending. This gave new meaning to the declaration by the angel in Revelation, *"Fallen, fallen is Babylon the great!"*

I believe the Lord is bringing a great division. But it's not going to fall upon the lines of Left versus Right. Instead we're going to see the formation of a united stand against the hidden Babylonian structures seeking to shift our nation from covenantal freedom into authoritarianism tied to idolatry. In the end the covenant nation will endure. And not only endure, but we will arise!

Sheep and Goat Nations—True Definition

In Exodus God brought His people into freedom from the gods of Egypt and the governance of Egypt—in other words, the spirit, and the structure. He brought them into the Covenant Land. And there He instructed His people to implement a governmental structure by which God is honored, and Holy Spirit can flow.

Through this a hidden piece of the puzzle is now coming into view. It's important to see. To genuinely secure America and the nations as a sheep nations instead of goat nations requires a shift in the spirit and structure—including the altar of dedication, the systems, and culture—from Babylon to Zion. The potential for this shift is secured by covenant, or covenant restoration, with God.

> *"You will no longer be termed forsaken, nor shall your land any more be termed desolate; but you shall be called Hephzibah, and your land Beulah, for the Lord delights in you and to Him your land shall be married"* (Isa. 62:4).

The Restoration Begins with You

Before we deal with nations or families, this restoration movement all begins with you. Remember how the high priest Joshua experienced God's hand of restoration in Zechariah 3. Joshua had to be cleansed of the sins of Babylon, the sins in which his forefathers engaged which led to the exile, before he could genuinely lead the restoration movement himself.

Please don't miss the significance of this. Joshua was first cleansed from the mantle tied to the sins of Babylon, especially idolatry. Then a new mantle—a new covering—was bestowed on him.

It is the same with you. The pursuit of healing and deliverance from generational cycles of sin is vital for your success. *This is how we divorce Babylon personally.* It's time to finally shut the

It's time to finally shut the gates of sabotage, and open the door to the preservation of godly legacy which secures a better future!

gates of sabotage, and open the door to the preservation of godly legacy which secures a better future!

And as we advance in this season, we are requesting the various expressions of today's prayer movement, nationally and internationally, to collaborate together to divorce Babylon corporately. We need a united front. We're going to be made strong by what every joint supplies. Together we're going to move with God's Spirit to deal with the spirit and structure of Babylon, even from its ancient roots. And what has been stolen, even an entire generation, will now be released!

Right now you can hear the resonance of the Breaker calling out. It's time. He is ready to bring forced compliance to the Kingdom decree. Let's divorce Babylon!

CHAPTER 12

THE FINISHING DECREE

"Come from the four winds, O breath, and breathe on these slain, so that they may live!" (Ezekiel 37 BSB).

THE WORLD'S MOST FAMOUS BATTLEGROUND is also perhaps the world's most famous graveyard. Har Megiddo, or Armageddon as it has come to be known, is a small mountain that overlooks the vast Jezreel Valley and serves strategically as a watchman's perch. The Egyptians, Canaanites, Philistines, Assyrians, Babylonian Empire, Persian Empire, Grecian Empire, Roman Empire, Muslim, and Crusader armies, and even Napoleonic armies, have all clashed there with enemies.

And in even more brutal battles, so have Elijah and Jezebel.

Naboth's vineyard was located in the Jezreel Valley. Not coincidentally, *Jezreel* means "God sows." It was there that Elijah prophesied the downfall of Jezebel after she arranged for Naboth's murder in order to steal his vineyard. *Naboth*, by the way, literally means "prophetic words." To a large extent, as shared in *White House Watchmen*, Jezreel is a vineyard of prophetic words, a vineyard of prophetic destiny.

Armageddon, and therefore the Jezreel Valley, is also the site identified by the apostle John as the host of the cataclysmic battle of the end of days. *"The war of the great day of God, the Almighty"* (Rev. 16:14).

But at present the Jezreel Valley is best known as the breadbasket of Israel. And Har Megiddo is a pleasant tourist stop en route to Nazareth and the Galilee, with a small cafeteria featuring very good ice cream, and a gift shop with hats that need an upgrade.

Ezekiel was exiled in Babylon when he was plucked up by a lock of his head and brought in the spirit to a valley of dry bones. Bible scholars cannot be sure, but due to both its history and prophesied future, many surmise it was the Jezreel Valley.

God told Ezekiel to look around and earnestly evaluate the condition of this *"vineyard of prophetic destiny that,"* that, in his experience, had become a graveyard. It was filled with the sun-bleached remains of countless brigades of soldiers. The valley was filled with dry bones.

"Son of man," God asked His friend, *"can these bones live?"*

Contending for Victory at Gettysburg

By mid-November 1863, the stench of rotting flesh had largely dissipated from the pastoral farmlands of Gettysburg, Pennsylvania, that in July had become the turning point of the entire Civil War. But the dead were still being buried. Sun-bleached bones remained scattered through the fields, even in the graveyard being prepared for an upcoming dedication. The bloodstained village in southern Pennsylvania seemed the unlikeliest place to encounter the Living God.

Abraham Lincoln stepped solemnly off the train and tucked away in the home of his host. It was at Gettysburg that he completed his simple address to dedicate the Soldiers' National Cemetery. Until arriving, the "finishing decree" of his address had proven elusive.

Can these bones live? Perhaps the president had received a battlefield visitation similar to Ezekiel. Because what he decreed over the nation after viewing the grounds was hauntingly similar to Ezekiel's sentiments. In the midst of the most divisive years of American history, President Lincoln chose the imagery of the born-again experience to decree that our nation must and will have a born-again experience. Nothing else could resurrect the broken land.

"That this Nation, under God, shall have a new birth of freedom; and that government, of the people, by the people, and for the people, shall not perish from the earth."

Victory and national healing were existential passions Lincoln had prayed for throughout the war, especially over the Battle of Gettysburg.

"In the pinch of your campaign up there," Lincoln recalled to a close friend and military leader, "when everybody seemed panic-stricken, and nobody could tell what was going to happen, oppressed by the gravity of our affairs, I went into my room one day and locked the door and got down on my knees before the Almighty God and prayed to Him mightily for victory at Gettysburg. I told Him this was His war and our cause, His cause, but that we couldn't stand another (defeat)."

Lincoln then confessed to his friend about a covenant he had made. "I then and there made a solemn vow to Almighty God that if he would stand by our boys at Gettysburg, I would stand by Him. And He did, and I will. And after that, I don't know how it was and I can't explain it, but soon a sweet comfort crept into my soul that things would go all right at Gettysburg, and this is why I had no fears."[1]

Maybe it's not a coincidence that Gettysburg became the turning point of the entire Civil War after Lincoln made covenant with God. Perhaps the greatest president of our nation proved that covenant unlocks turnaround, deliverance from adversaries, even for the nation. *"The covenant I have made with you, you shall not forget... and He will deliver you from the hand of all your adversaries"* (2 Kings 17:38-9).

The Finishing Decree

Let's return now to Ezekiel's valley of dry bones so we can take a closer look at the "finishing decree." If you're like me, you're going to gain a lot of clarity here that cuts through the confusion of making and manifesting decrees from the Lord. It will prove to be a very practical final lesson.

As you recall, God asked Ezekiel if the bones in the valley could live. In turn the prophet, overwhelmed by what he was seeing and experiencing, replied simply, "Oh Lord, only You know."

The word of the Lord then came. Make a decree!

> *Again He said to me, "Prophesy over these bones and say to them, 'You dry bones, hear the word of the Lord.' This is what the Lord God says to these bones: 'Behold, I am going to make breath enter you so that you may come to life. And I will attach tendons to you, make flesh grow back on you, cover you with skin, and put breath in you so that you may come to life; and you will know that I am the Lord.'"*
>
> *So I prophesied as I was commanded; and as I prophesied, there was a loud noise, and behold, a rattling; and the bones came together, bone to its bone. And I looked, and behold, tendons were on them, and flesh grew and skin covered them; but there was no breath in them* (Ezekiel 37:4-8).

When Ezekiel prophesied he saw an immediate manifestation of virtually everything God had told him to decree. A loud noise, then a rattling, pierced the airwaves with the sound of awakening. Bones came together. Tendons formed. Muscles formed. Skin was reconstituted to cover the bodies.

But despite prophesying twice about the breath of life returning, Ezekiel saw no breath fill the resurrected soldiers.

Can I say this? God wants you—expects you—to keep track of the progress of your prophetic words and decrees. He wants to hear from you a truthful evaluation.

And if we are honest, many times it seems the manifestation of these words only go so far. It's really exciting to see the initial burst. But then it becomes frustrating and sometimes embarrassing when the manifestation does not express the fullness of the promise decreed. These turnarounds are meant to be completed.

In Ezekiel's case, an earnest evaluation was met with God's direction for Ezekiel to prophesy again. A finishing decree!

"Prophesy to the breath, prophesy, son of man, and say to the breath, 'The Lord God says this: "Come from the four winds, breath, and breathe on these slain, so that they come to life."'" So I prophesied as He commanded me, and the breath entered them, and they came to life and stood on their feet, an exceedingly great army (Ezekiel 37:9-10).

Boom.

Until praying over this chapter I had not really perceived this pattern, nor had I ever heard the phrase "finishing decree." Then suddenly it was before me. If you've ever struggled with the need to watch over the decrees you have made, to continue praying and prophesying into what you've already decreed, this is for you.

Don't believe the enemy's lies that you have missed it, or that your authority in Christ has somehow been

> ...many times it seems the manifestation of these words only go so far. In Ezekiel's case, an earnest evaluation was met with God's direction for Ezekiel to prophesy again. A finishing decree!

compromised. Remember it was the Lord who brought you into this valley of bones in the first place! Relate to Him in honesty, evaluating where you are in your project. Tell Him what needs to be done to complete the turnaround. And let the Lord fill your mouth with His finishing decree!

Vision—Whirlwinds from the Throne

To more fully appreciate Ezekiel's graveyard miracle, it's important to understand a few dynamics. Despite popular belief to the contrary, Ezekiel was not prophesying to atmospheric winds in the natural. No wind, not even an ocean breeze, has the power to resurrect the dead. Though I'll take an ocean breeze as often as possible.

Instead, Ezekiel was prophesying to the winds of Heaven. To the divine Breath. The same breath that was breathed into Adam to make him a living soul was breathed into these dry bones. Each resurrected structure received resuscitated life. And an entire army arose.

The Lord gave me a picture of this two decades ago. I actually saw Jesus as the Ancient of Days. The fire over His countenance was so bright that I could not make out His features. As I looked on Him, I heard the phrase "the shining of the Ancient of Days."

Unexpectedly, Jesus bowed low by the crystal sea, and plunged His face into the water. Immediately the entire sea of glass lit up with overwhelming, blinding brilliance. Jesus then blew His breath into the sea. Whirlwinds immediately began to form, combining the substance of holy fire with the crystal clarity of the sea of glass and the very breath of His Spirit. I saw these whirlwinds from above then below. And when they touched the earth, a massive awakening began to sweep the land. Life from the dead!

Watch for these awakening winds to blow over the next few years. Even over historic battlefields such as Gettysburg, Shiloh, Wounded

Knee, Yorktown, Lexington, Valley Forge, and even the Jezreel Valley. They have been marked by war. But in Jesus, many battlefields that became graveyards are now being marked for awakening.

What battlefield do you want to see awakened? What breakthroughs only made it halfway through the gateway of your spheres?

In the midst of a graveyard, God set in Ezekiel's mouth a decree from the throne, to declare back to the throne, which compelled Heaven's substance into the earth. *Come from the four winds, O breath! Breathe on these slain that they may live, and the cause in Christ they gave their lives for would be fulfilled.*

Like Ezekiel, if you want to see powerful results, don't just decree from earth. Take your seat with Christ before the throne. Decree what He shows you to decree. Even speak to the vast resources of Heaven's storehouse, and command Heaven's substance to come and complete the turnaround.

Complete the Turnaround

Moses released a finishing decree. Actually, it was the same one he spoke to Pharaoh nine times before. Let My people go! But on the tenth time the decree was released, the turnaround was secured. A freedom movement burst forth.

Jesus had to release a finishing decree for one of His miracles to fully materialize. He was praying over a blind man. After the first effort, the man's reply was, *"I see men like trees walking."* Jesus prayed again. And the man received his full sight. *"Then again He laid His hands on his eyes; and he looked intently and was restored, and began to see everything clearly"* (Mark 8:25).

Elijah released a finishing decree as well. The prophet found it was a whole lot easier to see the heavens shut by divine decree than to open the heavens again. Elijah declared what he perceived in the spirit—*"I hear the sound of the abundance of rain!"* He then travailed in prayer until the rain actually came.

Elijah's servant checked the skies three separate times before the miracle finally materialized. Finally, a cloud the size of a man's hand appeared. The prophet then knew it was finished, and rain was on its way.

You will know too. Whether your prayer project is over children who need Jesus or a church needing resuscitation or a turnaround for the nation, Jolene and I want to admonish you not to cease standing until the turnaround decree God gave you is fully established. You will know when it materializes, and the results will pass the toughest of scrutiny.

That said, it's time to prophesy to your world. Release the decree. Complete the turnaround!

The closing sentence of Lincoln's Gettysburg Address is a powerful finishing decree for our season. Look over the dry bones of the turnaround God began in your life and make it your own. Decree over your children. Decree over your church. Decree to your nation! Because it's time to complete the turnaround. Covenantally and governmentally, we decree the blowing again of the breath of God. *Come from the four winds, O breath. Breathe on these slain, that they may live!*

"That this Nation, under God, shall have a new birth of freedom; and that government of the people, by the people, and for the people shall not perish from the earth."

New Birth of Freedom—Beginning in 2022

The door now stands open. What does this New Birth of Freedom look like? Here are twelve defining characteristics, largely explored through the book.

1. The global release of the Daniel 7:22 Turnaround Movement, and Turnaround Decrees, in all of its facets. Isaiah 54 is a defining expression of the turnaround God is granting in this day. *"Sing o barren woman! More are the children of the desolate woman than the children of the married wife. Spring forth! Your children will be taught of the Lord. They will possess nations and restore desolate habitations. Great will be their peace!"*

2. *"I will contend with the one who contends with you, and I will save your children!"* Massive contending prayer and Spirit-breathed decrees will turn the hearts of the fathers back to the children, and the hearts of the children to their fathers, and will be met with unusual intervention by God in rescue and redemption. The time is now. Remember—the Breaker brings forced compliance to the Kingdom decree!

3. Included in this turnaround movement is a resurgence of healing and deliverance from present and generational bondages.

4. The emergence of Zion thrones, of Kingdom thrones with a breaker anointing from the Lord to overcome Babylon thrones. Innovation belongs to the Kingdom! God is releasing an anointing to possess and secure the inheritance He ordained for you.

5. Covenant restoration realigns nations with the Lord Jesus Christ and unlocks His commanded blessing. Genuine covenant with the Lord becomes a primary demarcation between sheep and goat nations.

6. The door stands open for the completion of the turnaround intended by the Lord for the United States that perpetuates the freedom originally entrusted to the nation by covenant. Including election innovations that protect the integrity

of America's representational government and balance of power. A new era of victory has been decreed, and it still stands. The halls of government will be impacted. Awakening and common resolve will cause the true Spirit of America to soar.

7. The amplification of God's covenant covering over His Covenant People. Individuals, families, spheres, regions, and nations will experience His supernatural covering and deliverance from adversaries.

8. Shift to LIFE—from a covenant with death empowering a culture of death to a covenant of LIFE empowering a culture of life. *From abortion to awakening.* This includes annulling the Exodus 1:22 covenant with death against an entire generation.

9. The unlocking of another Jesus revolution that will sweep through this generation like an unstoppable train—a Glory Train. Dry bones will live! Multitudes will be birthed into the Kingdom and mentored into mature kings and priests before the Lord. Watch Alaska! Hawaii turns. The door is open for New England. Philadelphia has been known for cheesesteaks, but it's now going to be known for its shakes. Georgia fulfills its destiny as the reconstitution state. God is arising in the storm winds of the south! By the way, this Jesus revolution includes a massive underground revival in the US military and intelligence communities, in all the respective branches, in the midst of a shakeup. It will even spill over into diplomatic circles.

10. As Jolene prophesied so clearly, it is now time for the unsealing and releasing of key revelation reserved for the end times. Hear this with hearing ears. The door to Daniel 7 is open.

And the scrolls reserved for this time stand ready for the unsealing.

11. Movements birthed during the time period surrounding 9-11-01 will receive a fresh revitalization from the Lord in this season. Throne room winds come forth for this! Let's call forth the EXPERTS—including God's Eliakims—into their positions.

12. The reemergence of the forerunner spirit, turning the hearts of the fathers to the children, and the hearts of the children to their fathers. Note that fullest expression of this calling is specifically reserved for the era before the "great and terrible day of the Lord." Just as John the Baptist came in the spirit and power of Elijah as a forerunner of Jesus' first coming, God is now raising up forerunners expressing this dimension of Holy Spirit fire in preparation for Jesus' great return.

The mandate is a marker. Which casts Turnaround Tuesday, now a global movement, in a whole new light. No King but Jesus.

"Behold, I am going to send you Elijah the prophet before the coming of the great and terrible day of the Lord. He will turn the hearts of the fathers back to their children and the hearts of the children to their fathers, so that I will not come and strike the land with complete destruction" (Malachi 4:5-6).

"And it is he who will go as a forerunner before Him in the spirit and power of Elijah, to turn the hearts of fathers back to their children, and the disobedient to the attitude of the righteous, to make ready a people prepared for the Lord" (Luke 1:17).

Sign of the Burning Lamp

John the Baptist was sent in the spirit and power of Elijah to prepare the way for Jesus from His birth. You will see many in this era raised up and sent in the spirit and power of Elijah to prepare the way for Jesus' Second Coming. As of the "time gate" 2022, we are in a season of the reemergence of the forerunner spirit. Prepare the way of the Lord!

John the Baptist, who first came in the spirit and power of Elijah, was called by Jesus *"the burning and shining lamp"* (John 5:35). And just as a burning lamp appeared on the scene to prepare the way for His first coming, so many burning lamps are now being prepared to shine the way for Messiah's return. In a very real way, *the burning lamps themselves* become God's finishing decree.

So in a *Back to the Future* kind of way, let's end right where we began. A prophetic father named Zechariah was keeping watch over the restoration process from Babylon to Zion. Due to overwhelming resistance by the deep state of his day, the rebuilding of the Temple had largely ceased. There was no longer any resistance to the resistance.

Then, as recorded in Zechariah 4, God roused Zechariah from slumber and declared that it was now time to complete the turnaround. An angel who spoke to him in a former season returned and awakened the prophet from slumber. In process, this same angel reawakened in him the promises and dreams God had put in his heart.

As a sign of this resurgence, the Lord showed Zechariah a burning lamp in Heaven. This lamp was perpetually resourced with fresh oil from two olive trees on either side of it.

Watch this now...

The burning lamp itself became a finishing decree!

I prophesy to you that the Lord is releasing His burning lamps today as a sign that it is now time to finish the work. Restoring the hearts of the fathers to the children, and the children to their fathers. Completing the turnaround that He has initiated in former seasons.

You are among the burning lamps. Your light itself is God's finishing decree. *"Not by might, nor by power, but by My Spirit, says the Lord of hosts!"* (Zech. 4:6).

You might remember that the Maccabees experienced a measure of the miracle prophesied by Zechariah. Hanukkah, or the Feast of Dedication, celebrates this victory. The strongest military alliance in the known world had invaded Jerusalem and occupied the Temple of the Lord, snuffing out the fire and even defiling it through worship to Baal.

Against all odds this band of spiritual revolutionaries engaged the resistance and retook their desolate heritage. They relit the menorah, reconsecrating the Temple to the Lord. The burning lamp then became a symbol of restored covenant with Him, welcoming back His presence.

But there was only enough oil for the fire to burn one day. Miraculously, the Temple menorah burned for eight days consecutively, until a fresh supply of oil could be secured.

Be His burning lamp. By decree of the Lord, I declare that you too will be resourced with a perpetual supply of oil. Provision in the Spirit and the natural to blaze brightly, regardless of circumstances!

The Maccabees relit their menorah in the very face of tyranny. So did Rabbi Posner and his wife, celebrating

> ...your light itself will bear witness to God's resistance to the hatred, injustice, and subjugation the enemy seeks to impose on our world. Resistance to the resistance. Shine brightly. Shine courageously.

Hanukkah when they lit their menorah in their window directly across from a large Nazi flag.

For some of you, this same measure of devotion will be required. Like the Maccabees, like Daniel in Babylon or the Posners in the face of Nazi totalitarianism, your light itself will bear witness to God's resistance to the hatred, injustice, and subjugation the enemy seeks to impose on our world. Resistance to the resistance.

Shine brightly. Shine courageously. Let your candle light a thousand. Let your fire be a witness to Jesus' devotion to you, your devotion to Him, and His unyielding faithfulness to His covenant promise to complete the turnaround. Write the decree. And above all, dare to be His finishing decree!

No King but Jesus...

About
Jon & Jolene Hamill

WASHINGTON, DC NATIVES JON AND JOLENE HAMILL love to see God bring turnarounds into the lives of individuals, families, churches, and governmental spheres. Founders of Lamplighter Ministries, they minister extensively throughout the United States as well as Israel and many nations. In addition, they have served as advisors and intercessors for many governmental leaders.

Jon and Jolene have authored four books, including *Crown and Throne* (2013), *Midnight Cry* (2017), *White House Watchmen* (2020), and *Turnaround Decrees* (2022). In addition, their prophetic teachings have appeared on the Elijah List, in *Charisma Magazine* and other publications. Their online blog LAMPostings is focused on sharing real-time prophetic revelation and prayer points from Washington DC, and is regularly enjoyed by thousands.

Since 2012, Jon and Jolene have led a popular prayer call each Wednesday evening with the Lamplighter family nationwide. Their weekly home group in Pentagon City continues to flourish.

In 2022, they launched the Turnaround Tuesday movement, mobilizing the body of Christ to pray for turnarounds for our sons and daughters. Zoom broadcasts each Tuesday at 1pm ET bring inspiration, equipping, and prayer to multitudes globally on breakthrough prayer for our sons and daughters.

To connect please visit:
https://turnaroundtuesday.com

If you would like to receive real-time prophetic revelation from Washington DC, join calls, as well as receive email updates on ministry and prayer times, please visit: **https://lamplighterministries.net.**

NOTES

Chapter 1

1   Daniella J. Greenbaum, "Lighting Hanukkah Candles Under the Swastika's Shadow," The New York Times, December 12, 2017, https://www.nytimes .com/2017/12/12/opinion/happy-hanukkah-candles-swastikas.html.

Chapter 3

1   https://www.law.cornell.edu/wex/decree.

Chapter 4

1.   Reprinted from Jon and Jolene Hamill, "Consecrate 2022 Tonight! Plus One Year Ago Today...," *LAMPostings*, Lamplighter Ministries, January 5, 2022, https://jonandjolene.us/consecrate-2022-tonight-plus-one-year-ago-today/.

Chapter 8

1.   Bob & Bonnie Jones, "The Glory Train," *The Elijah List*.
2.   Chuck Pierce, *Interpreting the Times* (Charisma House: 2008), 5.

3. Note that portions of this vision were originally published in *"White House Watchmen,"* chapter 14.

4. Quotes compiled from https://screenrant.com/memorable-quotes-back-future-trilogy/.

Chapter 9

1. Henry Clay Trumbull, *The Threshold Covenant* (C. Scribner's: 1896), 240, qtd. in Hamill and Hamill, *White House Watchmen*, 80-81.

2. Hamill and Hamill, *White House Watchmen*, chapter 15.

Chapter 10

1. Composed by Dr. Jerry Mash with Apostle John Benefiel (OAPN, HAPN.US). Revised by Jon Hamill on 4-18-18. Ratified on 4-22-18 at Western Wall. The gavel of the Ancient of Days Fell!

Chapter 11

1. The verbiage is from my original notes, unedited except for grammar.

Chapter 12

1. Quoted in Stephen Mansfield, *Lincoln's Battle with God* (Thomas Nelson: 2012).

Journal